Jazz: From Its Origins to the Present

LEWIS PORTER
Rutgers University
Newark

MICHAEL ULLMAN
Tufts University

ED HAZELL

Prentice Hall
Englewood Cliffs, New Jersey 07632

Library of Congress Cataloging-in-Publication Data

Porter, Lewis.
   Jazz: from its origins to the present / by Lewis Porter and
Michael Ullman with Ed Hazell.
     p. cm.
   Discography: p.
   Includes bibliographical references and index.
   ISBN 0-13-092776-7 (case).–ISBN 0-13-512195-7 (paper)
   1. Jazz—History and criticism. I. Ullman, Michael
II. Hazzell, Ed. III. Title.
ML3506.P66 1992
781.65'09–dc20   92-37368
                                         CIP
                                       MN

Editorial/production supervision and interior design: Jordan Ochs
Acquisitions editor: Bud Therien
Editorial assistant: Lee Mamunes
Copyeditor: Mark Tobey
Prepress buyer: Herb Klein
Manufacturing buyer: Bob Anderson
Cover design: Ray Lundgren Graphics, LTD
Cover art: Duke Ellington and Billie Holiday. Courtesy of Rutgers
        Institute of Jazz Studies.

 © 1993 by Prentice-Hall, Inc.
A Simon & Schuster Company
Englewood Cliffs, New Jersey 07632

Printed in the United States of America
10 9 8 7 6 5 4 3 2 1

ISBN   0-13-512195-7 (paper)
ISBN   0-13-092776-7 (case)

Prentice-Hall International (UK) Limited, *London*
Prentice-Hall of Australia Pty. Limited, *Sydney*
Prentice-Hall Canada Inc., *Toronto*
Prentice-Hall Hispanoamericana, S.A. *Mexico*
Prentice-Hall of India Private Limited, *New Delhi*
Prentice-Hall of Japan, Inc., *Tokyo*
Simon & Schuster Asia Pte. Ltd., *Singapore*
Editora Prentice-Hall do Brasil, Ltda., *Rio de Janeiro*

Contents

Preface

We began this book in 1982 in response to what we—as fans, educators, authors, and, in Porter's case, a sometime performer—saw as a need for a literate, accurate, and up-to-date one-volume history of jazz and its major figures. We wanted that book to be musically sophisticated, inclusive and unbiased—to reflect our tastes and esthetic judgments certainly, but more importantly, to give a fair representation of the music that had the greatest impact on musicians and on the general public. When faced with a choice between an obscure personal favorite and a historically significant piece, we have opted for the latter.

We wanted our book to include musical examples, and enough prose explanation of those examples so that it would be readily comprehensible to the general reader. We would try to achieve a balance between talking about movements and talking about key musicians—some of whom, such as Duke Ellington and Coleman Hawkins, lived and played through many eras and styles of jazz. We wanted the book to reflect the original jazz history research we have done and continue to do, as well as the technical analysis of Lewis Porter and the interviewing and criticism of Michael Ullman. This original work distinguishes our book from most comparable histories.

As with most collaborations, our working methods have been complex. We began each chapter with a sketch by Porter, except for chapters 10 and 23 which Ullman initiated. The chapters shuttled between us several times after that, with corrections, additions, and revisions done by both authors, except for musical discussions which are in Porter's bailiwick. For chapters 17 through 22 and 24, critic Ed Hazell co-authored with Porter some extensive first drafts, providing generous amounts of material from his own research on modern jazz. Hazell also wrote the initial drafts of the glossary, bibliography, and discography.

This is the first jazz history book to be available also in CD-ROM, published by E-Book in cooperation with Prentice Hall. Lewis Porter has supervised the book's transformation into an interactive multimedia presentation. When the CD-ROM disc is played on a standard CD audio player, the student will hear the notated music examples as performed on a synthesizer. When it is played back on a computer, a world of possibilities opens up. The student will enjoy short video clips of jazz greats! The student may play each music example as a MIDI file, slow it down, then perform along with it. As with all CD-ROMs, the student may explore it in his or her own way by clicking on "buttons" that take the student here and there.

There is one other publication associated with this history, an instructor's manual which is available to teachers of jazz history free upon request from Prentice Hall. The manual, almost 100 pages long, contains informal advice about teaching, sample questions for discussion, homework, tests, a listing of jazz mail order companies, and other information of value to educators.

□ □ □

We advise readers of this history to begin with Appendix 1, which describes the structural principles of jazz, a basic knowledge of which is presumed throughout the text. We also advise readers to purchase at least a few jazz recordings. This book is keyed to the Smithsonian Collection of Jazz, but can be used productively with any number of smaller collections available, some of which are described in the Instructor's Manual.

It is customary when writing down jazz performances from recordings to use special symbols that indicate how things are played. These are summarized in Appendix 2. Alex Sweeton, John O'Gallagher, Tom Varner and Ingrid Monson each transcribed about six examples from recordings. Jazz pianist Steve Ash was a tremendous help proofreading and editing over half of the examples. All music examples, regardless of their source, have been checked and edited by Porter, who takes responsibility for their final form. He has made some alterations in almost every instance, even in the case of lead sheets, to make the examples conform to the recorded performances.

Musical examples are in concert key unless otherwise noted; for bass and guitar, which are usually written an octave higher than they sound, the music is written at sounding pitch or will have a note that it "sounds 8vb" (an octave lower). Since we believe that no jazz solo exists in isolation from the other musicians playing, Porter has sometimes indicated on the music examples aspects of the accompaniments to give a fuller picture of each recording. For the same reason, the chord symbols are those actually played by the accompanists, rather than those implied in the transcribed solo line or found in lead sheets. Throughout the text as well, we have tried to pay more attention to the rhythm section than is usually given. The captions on the music examples are minimal, since they are always identified more fully in the text. Where a music example consists of a written theme, the year of composition (where known) or of first recording is given. The year given for improvised solos is that of the particular recording used, which in many cases is later than the year that the piece was written. The letters SCCJ after a cited recording mean that it appears in *The Smithsonian Collection of Classic Jazz* (revised edition), BBJ refers to *Big Band Jazz: From the Beginning through the Fifties*, and JP refers to the *Jazz Piano* boxed set, but we have not restricted our examples to these collections from the Smithsonian Institution. Other citations for recordings and literature are given briefly in the text, but will be found more completely in the Discography and Bibliography.

Where they have not been otherwise identified, the statements of musicians in this book come from interviews conducted by Michael Ullman. Within any quotations, bracketed words are our additions. Our Sidney Bechet chapter appeared in slightly different form in *The Black Perspective in Music*, Volume 16, No. 2 (Fall, 1988), and about half of the Armstrong chapter appeared in *Jazz Educators Journal*, Volume 22, No. 2 (1990). The Basie chapter appeared in different form in *The Missouri Review*, Volume 10, No. 1 (January 1987). Several short passages have been adapted from various pieces that Ullman contributed to the *Boston Phoenix*, *Boston Globe*, and *New Republic*.

The staff of the Institute of Jazz Studies at Rutgers University—Dan Morgenstern, Ed Berger, Vince Pelote, Don Luck, John Clement, Esther Smith and Fran Cosgrove—provided help with countless details over the years. About half of our photographs came from the Institute. We would also like to acknowledge Ingrid Monson for reading and commenting on chapters one through twelve, and Harriet Ullman for proofreading the text. Critic William Youngren provided helpful comments to Ullman on the Basie and Bechet chapters especially, while Porter received many helpful suggestions from Bill Kirchner, Joshua Berrett, Peter Pullman, Leonard Sayles, Dan Frank, and David Weiser. Porter is grateful to his wife Gail and to his brothers, Spence and Gilbert, for their constant support. We both owe many thanks to our extraordinarily enthusiastic—and patient—editor, Bud Therien, and to our production editor Jordan Ochs. For the CD-ROM edition, we thank Ron Woolridge, Fred Jones, Jessee Allread, Jim Donofrio, Roger East, Patrick Milligan, and Frank Gordon. Finally, we want to thank the musicians—from Benny Waters and Doc Cheatham to Dexter Gordon, Ornette Coleman and Pat Metheny—who consented to be interviewed. Their perspectives and insights are crucial to this book, which we hope reflects accurately the beliefs and practices of the jazz musicians whom we admire.

1 Introduction

"If you have to ask what it is," Louis Armstrong supposedly said, "you'll never know." Nevertheless, people have been asking about jazz since the second decade of this century. Jazz was first recorded in February 1917, when a quintet of white musicians from New Orleans, calling themselves the Original Dixieland Jazz Band, stepped into a New York studio to record two tunes, "Livery Stable Blues" and the "Dixie Jass Band One-Step" (two titles from January 1917 were not issued at the time). Later that year they were back in the studios, recording such numbers as the "Ostrich Walk," "Tiger Rag," and another version of "Livery Stable"—this time they called it the "Barnyard Blues." It's not coincidental that these titles have zoological implications: as introduced by the ODJB, jazz was a hepped-up, jittery music full of comic effects—horse whinnies, tiger roars, mooings and cowbells. Some listeners found the rhythms enlivening. Others feared their effects on mind and body. Jazz rhythms, or <u>jungle rhythms</u> as they were sometimes called, were held to cause various ills, including headaches and hypertension. Like marijuana, jazz was thought to destroy one's ability to concentrate.

The critics and music educators of the twenties who took notice of this new music tended to treat jazz as a passing fad or, if they feared it, as something like an infectious disease. Few seemed to understand the phenomenon they were discussing. Carl Engel, an ambivalent friend of the music, wrote in the August 1922 *Atlantic Monthly* that "jazz is upon us, everywhere," adding that, "as a state of mind," jazz is a "symptom, not malady," a symptom of some other indisposition in American culture. Quite rightly, Engel notes that jazz comes from the music of black America: He adds that it is "recklessly fantastic, joyously grotesque." To Engel, good jazz is a refinement of the "Negro style."

Music educator Edwin Stringham (*Musical Quarterly*, April 1926) saw jazz as, above all, an "educational problem." It provided "esthetical relaxation," presumably to those previously burdened with the task of interpreting more serious music. Stringham offered a definition of jazz, which he sees as the "utilization of a strongly marked rhythm of unusual nature . . . which may or may not be interwoven with two or more rather free contrapuntal parts." Stringham sees jazz as primarily a written music, as likely to be composed by Irving Berlin as to be created spontaneously by a Louis Armstrong. He admits it is rather strong stuff: He calls it a "germ" that must be watched and controlled, presumably by music educators. Repeatedly, early writers use this biological terminology. Jazz is potentially corrupting, Henry Gilbert warned in 1922, but he rather cheerily added, citing Mark Twain's cynical story "The Man Who Corrupted Hadleyburg" as evidence, that if people didn't go to the devil through jazz, they would find some other route, so there was probably no avoiding it.

There were musicians who saw promise in jazz. In 1924, *Etude Music Magazine,* after a note that said that it wasn't endorsing the music, devoted much of the August and September issues to the comments of prominent musicians on what it called "The Jazz Problem." Opinions varied, but bandleader and composer John Philip Sousa was intrigued by the music, with its "exhilarating rhythm, its melodic ingenuities." Composer Henry Gilbert found the musical effects of jazz "pregnant with suggestion for the serious American composer."

Some educators weren't worried about jazz, but not because they liked it. *The Musician,* a music teacher's journal, opened its May 1922 issue by declaring that jazz was dying, a diagnosis that has been repeated again and again in the music's history. "Its day—if it ever really had a day—is passing and teachers will have less and less of it to contend with," *The Musician* concluded. A year later, cornet player King Oliver made his first recordings, introducing a young Louis Armstrong to the world. Jazz, which developed in obscure ways around the turn of the century from the music of African-Americans in the South, was just beginning.

The early histories had a concise and attractive story to tell about its origins. Jazz, they said, was invented in New Orleans, after a worsening racial situation in that city forced the light-skinned "Creoles of color," whose musicians tended to be trained as well as skilled, in closer contact with the darker population uptown, where untrained players who could barely read music played a rough and ready improvised blues. Music of these uptown players was a kind of folk music; that of the downtowners, a light dance music (In this version there is rarely an attempt to define blues, folk or dance music). The combination was jazz, which moved north to Chicago and elsewhere after 1917, when Storyville, the vice district where much of the music was played, was closed at the urging of the United States Navy. Sailors were suffering from the crime and venereal disease that flourished in "the district," as New Orleans musicians called it.

Later research has complicated this story. Some New Orleans musicians travelled far and wide before 1917, and the exact repertoire of the different locales inside New Orleans is not so clear cut: certainly, black musicians as well as Creoles were playing dance music. Still, there remains considerable evidence that jazz did begin in and around New Orleans, if not in the bawdy houses of the red light district. Its most important early practitioners—King Oliver, Jelly Roll Morton, Sidney Bechet, Louis Armstrong—were from New Orleans. New Orleans was a unique place, unique in its complicated racial mix, in the many opportunities the city offered both to hear and play music, and in its tightly organized community of musicians. Elsewhere, people may have been playing something like jazz early in the music's history. They were certainly improvising on popular melodies. Nevertheless, black musicians have testified that what they were doing was not necessarily jazz, that the real thing was something else, that it came up from New Orleans, or was learned by imitating New Orleansians playing, live or on record. Doc Cheatham, a trumpet player born in Memphis in 1905, performed from his early teens in a church band. After playing marches and hymns and ragtime-influenced popular material, he and his friends would get together and improvise: "We called it playing jazz," he said. But it wasn't until he heard the 1921 recordings by Memphis trumpet man Johnny Dunn, who was himself exposed to New Orleans music, that, according to Cheatham, he discovered real jazz. To Cheatham, jazz was an identifiable style, not merely a word.

Saxophonist Benny Waters—he was later to play with King Oliver and Jelly Roll Morton—was born in Maryland in 1902. He told this story about his early experiences: "I was playing when I was six years old—the organ, or piano. I didn't hear much of nothing then except church music and singing, and my

Doc Cheatham at home, 1978. (Photo by Michael Ullman)

brothers and the things they were doing—that was more commercial. They played some classics and military band stuff . . . I came to Philadelphia when I was eight or nine . . . I played commercial music with my brothers. We were playing for rich people, parties and dances. We had stock arrangements [purchased sheet music] for the classics. For the other stuff, we didn't need them. Sometime it would be just my brother and I, and the piano and rhythm. He would play the melody and I would invent countermelodies. I was doing some improvising, but I wouldn't call it jazz."

Both Cheatham and Waters were improvising before they played what they would now call jazz, and both felt that jazz was an identifiable new music, different from the dance or popular-oriented music they had been playing. What was the new element? Perhaps it was the new way elements of earlier musics had come together. In his poetic way, black saxophonist and clarinetist Sidney Bechet, born in New Orleans in 1897, called the music "a lost thing finding itself," suggesting that jazz was the fulfillment of certain strands of earlier black musics. "It's like a man with no place of his own. He wanders the world and he's a stranger wherever he is; he's a stranger right in the place where he was born. But then something happens to him and he finds a place, *his* place" (*Treat it Gentle*, p. 48). Bechet tied the music to the black person's yearning for liberation and self-expression. Importantly, he believed that at some time in his childhood, the music found a home, that it came together decisively.

To the end of his life, Sidney Bechet continued to call his music "ragtime." He was offended by the original meaning of the word "jazz," and considered it a label that white people had attached to the "long song from the South" of his

Benny Waters around 1980. (Photo by Michael Ullman)

people. There have been many arguments since about the origin of the word "jazz." It seems possible that it does indeed derive from *orgasm*, which was already reduced to *jasm* by the mid-1800's, and which became *jazz* or *jass*, its primary meaning being sexual intercourse. The word also had, and has today, a more general meaning of energy, liveliness, as in "Let's jazz this up." The first known printed use of the word was in the *San Francisco Bulletin* in 1913. In his intriguing article, "Our Word Jazz" (*Storyville*, No. 50, Dec. 1973-Jan. 1974), Dick Holbrook quotes sportswriter "Scoop" Gleeson as praising a late-blooming player as "very much to the jazz." Later that year the same paper ran an article defining the word: "Anything that takes manliness or effort or energy or activity or strength of soul is 'jaz.' " (When a word is new, its spelling is often not yet standardized, so one finds various spellings of jazz in the early writings.)

Eventually the word became attached to music, definitively when the ODJB recorded in 1917. The word suggested the rhythmic liveliness of the music, which was certainly one of its crucial qualities. But ragtime, with its near constant, perky syncopation, was also lively. What distinguished jazz, at least in the eyes of some of its early practitioners, was its room for improvisation, and its potential seriousness: its soulfulness, to use a common phrase. Clarinetist Darnell Howard, who in his distinguished career played with James P. Johnson, Earl Hines, and Fletcher Henderson, said admiringly of the King Oliver band—a group dominated by New Orleans natives including Louis Armstrong—that they thought of themselves as artists.

Jazz, as we shall see, borrowed some of the procedures and forms of ragtime. It also borrowed something of the vocalistic expressiveness and profound intentions of the blues singers. From the beginning, jazz players wanted to "swing," to create a propulsive feeling of forward motion around a steady beat, a feeling which paradoxically best develops when musicians start to, in various ways, tug away from that steady beat without abandoning it entirely. Jazz players strived for their own readily identifiable sound or tone color. They have wanted to express *themselves*, but in the context of a communally made music. For this purpose, they formed bands. The earliest jazz and ragtime bands might have a fiddle, some winds, banjo or guitar, tuba or bass, but sometimes had no piano or drumset. By 1930, the instrumentation was becoming standardized. Jazz bands settled on a rhythm section of piano, bass, drums and optional guitar, to which were added any number of wind instruments.

The traditions of jazz, however they have been stretched, have never been forgotten. As Bechet said in *Treat It Gentle* (p. 202), "A musicianer could be playing it in London or Tunis, in Paris, in Germany. But no matter where it's played, you gotta hear it starting way behind you. There's the drum beating from Congo Square [in New Orleans] and there's the song starting in a field just over the trees. The good musicianer, he's playing *with* it and he's playing *after* it. He's finishing something. No matter what he's playing, it's the long song that started back there in the South."

What binds together the jazz of the twenties with that of the nineties is not the theories of the historians, but the beliefs and practices of the musicians. Perhaps one appeal of jazz is that it has a rich, available tradition, and yet it thrives on freedom and innovation. As pianist Thelonious Monk said, "Jazz and freedom go hand in hand. That explains it. There isn't any more to add to it. If I do add to it, it gets complicated. That's something for you to think about. You think about it and dig it. You *dig* it." In the following pages, we will certainly add to Monk's pithy statement, but we hope our discussions will send our readers back to the music as better listeners: The music, from King Oliver to Ornette Coleman and beyond, is there for us all to *dig*.

2 Beginnings

Although some musicians insisted they invented it (the Original Dixieland Jazz Band, for instance, and, with more reason, New Orleans pianist and composer Jelly Roll Morton), and although others seem to remember when it was first played and by whom (most commonly, by New Orleans cornetist Buddy Bolden around the turn of the century), jazz, it is certain, was not the simple and inevitable creation of a single band or person. It wasn't born and immediately recognized as a new creation. In fact, many New Orleans musicians called the new music by the older term *ragtime* to their dying day. It didn't even evolve in a straight line from its sources. It probably was never exactly a folk music, in the sense of a music played by amateurs. The first jazz players were mostly semi-professional musicians, who supplemented an income from day jobs with musical "gigs." Still it drew on various forms of folk music in the black community. Its elements were found in the rich, but relatively undocumented, music of late nineteenth century America. Its early practitioners were likely to have heard ragtime, but also marches, hymns, quadrilles and other dances in stock arrangements by brass bands or string bands or combinations of both. (Stock arrangements are published orchestrations of popular material, meant to be played by groups of varying skills and instrumentation. Many rags were published in stock arrangements, as were Sousa marches.) They could have heard blacks singing work songs, field hollers, spirituals and the precursors of blues, but they were aware of published popular songs as well. If they lived in New Orleans, they might have heard snatches of western classical music, or perhaps whole operas. In 1881, a black public school in New Orleans put on a production of Gilbert and Sullivan's comic opera *H.M.S. Pinafore.*

Until recently it was thought that the first jazz generation might have also observed some extraordinary exhibitions of African music and dance in New Orleans' Congo Square. But these performances, it now seems likely, stopped

7

√ much earlier than was previously believed, perhaps as early as 1835, so they could not have had a direct influence on jazz. (See Henry Kmen, "The Roots of Jazz and Dance in Place Congo: A Reappraisal.") Still, the jazz musicians might have heard something like African music in a modified form. And they certainly knew Latin American dances, which reflect African influences, because ragtime and early jazz piano pieces sometimes used the habanera dance rhythm, found in the tango, in the left hand. Therefore, jazz researchers, seeking to explain the origins of certain persistent characteristics of the music of black Americans—its rhythmic complexity, its blue notes and call-and-response patterns—have gone to African music as a source. Using available recordings and oral histories, they attempt to extrapolate back to the early 1800's, when many slaves were still first generation Africans. In his much admired book, *Early Jazz*, Gunther Schuller makes the extreme statement that "*every* musical element—rhythm, harmony, melody, timbre, and the basic forms of jazz—is essentially African in background and derivation." (See his chapter "The Origins" which leads up to this statement on page 62, and see also William Youngren's questioning of this position in "Analyzing Jazz," *Hudson Review*, Autumn 1969.)

Nevertheless, those who first listen to a recording of authentic African drumming, even those recordings recommended by Schuller, and then hear any recording of early jazz, will be surprised, not by the essential resemblances of the two, but by their obvious differences. Much of the music of West Africa, where many black Americans have ancestry, consists of songs accompanied by percussion. Often the music is meant to be danced to, as is much folk music throughout the world. Sometimes the drummers will be joined by musicians playing wooden flutes and tuned percussion instruments such as balafons, which are like marimbas. There is also music for wooden harp and for the guitar, a more recent addition. Paul Oliver, in his book *Savannah Syncopators*, suggests that more blacks were brought from string-playing areas than from drumming tribes. If he is right, it will be important to study these other types of music for possible connections with African-American styles.

The drum music can be fantastically complex rhythmically. Every instrument, including the voice, may have a part that, when added to the others, combines in a system of interlocking parts. Every part relates to a basic beat in different ways. Some clearly go along with it, some parts seem to work against the beat. Vocal parts may use some harmony in fourths or thirds, although there is no chord progression such as one finds in jazz or rock music. For the untrained listener, the problem in listening to authentic African music may simply be to identify the beat. That's hardly the case with early jazz. However brilliantly played, it jogs along to a readily identifiable beat, usually four beats to a measure.

There *are* parallels between some African music and African-American music. Some of the scales used in West Africa create a music that resembles the
√ blues. Some of the vocal techniques of the Africans remind us of the blues with its "bent" notes that slide up or down to a basic pitch, its sometimes nasal, wailing timbre. Listening to Negroes singing spirituals in the 1860's, Lucy

McKim Garrison noted that the singing abounded in "slides from one note to another" (Eileen Southern, ed., *Readings in Black American Music,* p. 152). Jazz players too have always been noted for the way they bend notes and for their individual, sometimes gruff, tone on their instruments. But they are more likely to have learned these techniques from early African-American singers than from a direct African source.

African music is a social music meant frequently to accompany dancing, but also work, religious ceremonies and secular events. Early observers of blacks making music in America remark repeatedly that these people seemed always to be singing, especially at work. A gentleman from Delaware, Lucy McKim Garrison's uncle, notes that "some of the best *pure negro* songs I have heard were those that used to be sung by the black stevedores [men who unload ship cargoes] . . . at the wharves in Philadelphia and Baltimore" (*Readings in Black American Music,* p. 153). Jelly Roll Morton recalled with fondness the songs of the stevedores in New Orleans around the turn of the century. Later, and as a result of the influence of white culture, blacks stopped singing in some of these contexts. Scholar Lawrence Levine has opined that many black Americans learned, in the years after the Civil War, to make less music, whether in imitation of whites, as a sign of dignity, or because their working conditions had changed. He says: "Silence was unquestionably one of the fruits of acculturation" (*Black Culture and Black Consciousness,* p. 203). Nonetheless, work songs survived well into the twentieth century—some have been recorded.

It was impossible for African music to survive unchanged in America, given the conditions in which African-Americans were placed. An ensemble music, where all parts are important and must be played accurately as handed down orally—not improvised, except in part by the master drummer—African music depends on a stable community, if only so that players may learn their parts. The music reflects a shared world view which must have changed with the radical dislocation that slavery caused: some slave owners deliberately tried to mix up blacks from different tribes so as to destroy their native traditions—traditions that suggested a solidarity that might prove threatening to white supremacy. Few blacks arrived in the United States from Africa after January 1, 1808, when the slave trade was declared illegal by the Federal government (several northern states, as well as Great Britain, passed similar laws around the same time). Some four generations intervened between the time when most blacks were brought to this country and the time, around the turn of the century, when jazz came together. Once here, slaves were generally denied the drums that were central to the music of their homeland. The drums, with which Africans could communicate in a language incomprehensible to their overseers, were considered subversive.

But blacks certainly kept various songs, dances and musical practices alive, although they adapted them to their new conditions. They adapted what they absorbed from white culture as well, making spirituals out of hymns, and influencing hymn writing in turn by the early 1800's. Around 1900, they combined the laments of field hollers with the satire of some of their work songs, to make the various kinds of country blues. Their music seemed to contain recognizable African traits, even after many blacks were no longer able to speak African languages, and when some among them had switched to European instruments and European musics. Recalling his Civil War regiment of black soldiers, abolitionist Thomas W. Higginson describes a ring shout, a religious celebration in which his soldiers would shuffle, barely moving their feet in a circle, while singing, "one of their quaint, monotonous, endless, negro-Methodist chants, with obscure syllables recurring constantly, and slight variations interwoven, all accompanied with a regular drumming of the feet and clapping of the hands, like castanets" (*Readings in Black American Music*, p. 176). Like others who heard this kind of event, Higginson was struck by the "monotonous" melodies on one hand, and by the dancers' "perfect time" on the other. (The primacy of rhythm, a lasting characteristic of black American music, was noticeable from the beginning. But no one would accuse Louis Armstrong, for instance, of producing "monotonous" melodies.) Even Sidney Bechet, a Creole born in urban New Orleans, remembered that the first music he made was with his family: They "beat time with their hands on drums" (*Treat It Gentle*, p. 2).

Such practices as ring shouting probably did survive in some rural areas, such as the Georgia Sea Islands, into the twentieth century. But we know of no jazz player who has said that he participated in one, although New Jerseyian James P. Johnson named an early piece after them: "Carolina Shout." Indeed, there is reason to believe that the earliest jazz people would not have known ring shouting. Cornetist Buddy Bolden (1877-1931), who lived and died in New Orleans, was said to have had the first jazz band: His group was made up of city men.

Still, the observations of Higginson and others indicate a sometimes overlooked fact, that many whites were fascinated from the beginning by the music black men and women were making around them; by its unexpected timbres and by its rhythmic life and apparent spontaneity. One indication of this fascination that would have an influence on jazz is the minstrel show. Minstrel shows got their start in the early nineteenth century, when white actors and musicians began to darken their faces with cork and imitate, or caricature, the dances, songs and humor of blacks whom they had observed. By the 1820's these shows had developed their own conventions and their own stereotyped characters; such as Jim Crow, a careless southern slave, and Dandy Jim, a ridiculously affected urban black. These caricatures drew on a burgeoning tradition of nineteenth-century American humor, which specialized in stock characters such as the wily Yankee, the dumb country boy—or conversely the cunning one who outsmarts the city slicker. Clayton Henderson writes, in *The New Grove Dictionary of American Music*, that blackface minstrelsy reached its height of popularity from around 1840 to 1870. By then its patterns were set. The shows were introduced by a humorous master of ceremonies, and used instruments such as a banjo, tambourine, bones—actual bones or flat sticks used as percussion—violin and accordion. The minstrels presented a medley of songs—"Dixie" by Dan Emmett was a hit—dances and humorous skits.

After the Civil War, minstrel troupes of black performers appeared and thrived. Their performances were surely full of interesting irony: These were black musicians and dancers who performed in organizations modelled on white minstrel shows that caricatured the life of African-Americans. Nonetheless, the shows helped train and establish the careers of black musicians. By 1890, according to Clayton Henderson, "Blacks were firmly established in American show business." These shows continued on a lesser scale into the twentieth century, when they died out or merged into vaudeville. It is notable that, as did other blues singers, Ma Rainey got her start in a minstrel show, F.S. Wolcott's "Rabbit Foot Minstrels." Bessie Smith joined the same show in 1912. Lester Young, Cootie Williams and others performed in such shows. The minstrel shows helped make professionals out of talented black performers, and spread the various forms of African-American music.

Sidney Bechet, who saw jazz as a spirit rather than merely a genre of music, said that the music started with the Emancipation Proclamation when the ex-slaves looked to their music as a guide:

> They needed the music more than ever now; it was like they were trying to find out in this music what they were supposed to do with this freedom . . . they had learned it wasn't just white people the music had to reach to, nor even to their own people, but straight out to life and to what a man does with his life when it finally *is* his" (*Treat It Gentle*, p. 50).

The music was used by those most involved with it to discover how they could feel and what they could do. It provided a means of self-expression unavailable to slaves, and it was a means of self-discovery through which a people healed themselves and found out what they could be. Bechet heard the same rhythm, he said, in spirituals as in ragtime and in what we have come to call jazz. Jazz, he continued, "wasn't spirituals or blues or ragtime, but everything all at once, each one putting something over on the other" (*Treat It Gentle*, p. 48). The mixed quality of jazz — its use of other genres such as the blues and ragtime — has been a feature of the music from the beginning.

RAGTIME

It has been thought that jazz was the product of a reasonably straight line of development, that the blues and various folk musics were created first, and that ragtime came later, only to be replaced by jazz. Now it seems likely that ragtime was developing alongside of blues and jazz, which did indeed mature later. As Gunther Schuller has written, "Jazz in its several early forms was contained within ragtime from the very beginnings, with the boundaries often overlapping and at times probably even interchangeable" (Schuller, "Rags, the Classics, and Jazz," in J.E. Hasse, ed., *Ragtime: Its History, Composers, and Music*). Early, unnotated *rags*, the ancestors of published ragtime compositions, were often at least partly improvised. Later, bands which played stock ragtime arrangements may have improvised a little as well.

Ragtime as it has evolved—there are of course few traces left of the music that preceded written ragtime—is primarily a piano or vocal music. (Many more ragtime songs became popular than piano rags, but the latter have always had more prestige.) Ragtime as a recognized genre of piano music, the ragtime of Scott Joplin and James Scott and Joseph Lamb, is really the final flowering of a style of music that was formalized by these masters. Most of its traits—its characteristically syncopated themes, its reliance on appealing folk, or folklike, melodies—were probably created by itinerant pianists and other musicians. (A serious argument has been made about the importance of banjo styles to ragtime. See Lowell Schreyer, "The Banjo in Ragtime," in Hasse, *op. cit.*) Ragtime, according to John Hasse, was "in development some ten or twenty years before the first ragtime song, so labeled, was published in 1896." It was developing, in other words, just before the time most observers have said jazz was developing and the blues was being formalized. He estimates that "the process of ragging an existing melody, though not under that name, dates back to at least the 1870's" (Hasse, "Ragtime: From the Top," in Hasse, *op. cit.*). Jelly Roll Morton remembers "ragging" light classical numbers: he would take a theme, add the characteristic bass and filigree ornamentations of the ragtime style and create not exactly a new work, but an amusing, irreverent comment on one that already

Scott Joplin around 1911. (Courtesy Rutgers Institute of Jazz Studies)

existed. He illustrated this process on his 1938 recordings for the Library of Congress with a theme from "Il Trovatore" by Verdi.

The music of Scott Joplin and his peers was a formalized music that these men and women created from largely folk material, using European classical piano techniques found in, among others, Robert Schumann, Emmanuel Chabrier, and the New Orleans composer Louis Moreau Gottschalk. Joplin, whose "Maple Leaf Rag," published in 1899, was ragtime's first great hit, was a classically trained pianist with a wide exposure to popular piano styles. In his early youth, he made a living as an itinerant pianist. His rags are sophisticated compositions involving several themes in different keys and often a considerable amount of counterpoint between the hands. They exhibit harmonic creativity as well as great rhythmic vitality and delightfully appealing melodies. The form of rags came from <u>marches</u>. In fact, Joplin's first two published compositions are marches that appeared in 1896: his "Combination March," and his "Great Crush Collision [March]," which seems to memorialize a train accident, although historians cannot figure out which one. It includes an imitation of the rushing trains, and train whistles—first slow and drawn out as the trains approach a crossing, and then quick and staccato before the collision, which is signalled by a big two-handed F^7 chord in the bass.

Ragtime composers took readily to the form of the march. That form was convenient and it was well known to most Americans through the ever-popular compositions of bandleader <u>John Philip Sousa</u> (1854-1932). The main themes of Sousa's "High School Cadets" (1890) are shown in the example. (See music example.)

Example 2–1.
"High School Cadets." Beginning of each theme, after the introduction.

"High School Cadets" begins with a four bar introduction, and then the form is straightforward: Each theme is played twice, beginning in the key of D^b

for the introduction (not shown) and for themes A and B, then changing to the key of G♭ for themes C and D. So, the form is Introduction, AABBCCDD. The main themes of "Maple Leaf Rag," named after a club in Sedalia, Missouri where Joplin appeared, are shown in the example. (In this case we give both hands since this was written for the piano.) (See music example.)

*=syncopation
Example 2–2.
Scott Joplin, "Maple Leaf Rag" (1899). Beginning of each theme.

A player piano roll of "Maple Leaf Rag" made by Joplin in 1916 may be heard on *The Smithsonian Collection of Classic Jazz* (henceforth SCCJ). The form of the rag is AABBACCDD, with no introduction, and it differs from the march in the reprise of A just before going into C, and in the fact that the last theme goes back to the original key. One finds various other sequences of four themes in marches as well as rags. Sousa's "Stars and Stripes Forever" is Intro, AAB-BCDCDC, and his "Manhattan Beach" is Intro, ABCDD (with the whole thing repeated), while Joplin's "The Chrysanthemum" is AABBACCDDC, and his

"Felicity Rag" is AABBACC Bridge AA. Still, rags such as "Maple Leaf Rag" retain the essential aspects of the march: the use of several themes or "strains" in 16-bar sections which are increasingly active and exciting, until the key change after the first two themes. (In both marches and rags, this key change frequently signals the entrance of a gentler theme.) Notice also Joplin's marking *Tempo di marcia*, which means "march tempo," and the word *Trio* before the third theme, as in a march.

The march has virtually no syncopation—accents off of the first and third beats of a measure—but consists almost entirely of quarter and half notes on the beat. The rag, with its origins in African-American folk music, is syncopated from bar one. (See the asterisks on the above examples, which indicate obvious syncopations.) The B theme of "Maple Leaf" begins with the same rhythm as the A, but where the A section moves on, the B develops that rhythm. Although the stereotype about ragtime is that the left hand plays a tuba-like "oompah" bass, here the left-hand part is relatively complex: When you listen, you realize that the "oompah," where present, is in the background, and elsewhere what is played are sophisticated variations of that device. These rhythmic elements clearly distinguish the rag from its formal model, the march. Still, it is no wonder, considering the similarities in form and harmony between rags and marches, that Sousa played and recorded classic rags and that an important part of the repertoire of early black brass bands was marches. Other bands shared that repertoire. In March 1909, the U.S. Marine Band recorded an arrangement of "Maple Leaf Rag."

THE BLUES

If jazz used the form and some of the devices of marches and ragtime, it took some things just as important from the country blues: an approach to improvisation, a predilection towards conveying strong emotion, towards "telling a story," and an aesthetic that rewards a musician who tells a story in an individual way. The origins of the blues are as murky as are the origins of jazz. Most likely the blues was crystallizing in the last decade of the nineteenth century, a little before witnesses said the first jazz was being played. The publishing history of the blues begins in the twentieth century. Twelve-bar blues strains appeared in published rags as early as 1904, and scholar Lawrence Gushee has discovered a piece entitled "I've Got the Blues" which was published in New Orleans in 1908. With his publication of "Memphis Blues" in 1912 and "St. Louis Blues" in 1914, W.C. Handy started a fad for the blues. He readily acknowledged that his sources were black folk singers. He wrote that in 1892 he heard "shabby guitarists picking out a tune called 'East St. Louis.' It had numerous one-line verses and they would sing it all night: 'I walked all the way from old East St. Louis, and I didn't have but one po' measly dime' " (W.C. Handy, *Father of the Blues*, pp. 147-148). Jelly Roll Morton recalled hearing a woman named Mamie Desdoumes sing what he named "Mamie's Blues" around the turn of the century: it is a standard 12-bar blues, with a repeated first line and rhyming second line, so it is fairly certain that the 12-bar, AAB rhyme scheme (see Appendix 1) was known in New Orleans early. Texas blues singer Mance Lipscomb has said that he heard blues as a child—he was born in 1895. On the other hand, James P. Johnson said that he didn't hear any blues in the Northeast until 1912.

The early country blues singers, who most frequently accompanied themselves on guitars, probably did not think in terms of the 12-bar form that became standard. In the 1920's and later, there are numerous recorded examples of odd phrase lengths in blues. A country blues singer could extend a phrase or clip a rhythm because he or she was usually a soloist. Charlie Patton (b. 1897) has been called the founder of the delta blues. On his "Pony Blues," Patton injected a bar with six beats after the second line of his first chorus. As his own accompanist, he had the freedom to do so.

But the needs of a band, or of a singer accompanied by a guitarist or band, were different. Country blues singer Texas Alexander (b. circa 1880) often recorded with a guitarist, who sometimes appears to have difficulty when the singer spontaneously extends or shortens lines. A later bluesman, John Lee Hooker (b. 1917), employed the same freedom from the start of his career to the present. The Muddy Waters band seems to be struggling to follow him on their record together from 1966, *Live at Cafe au Go-Go* (Bluesway).

If a band were to improvise a blues, it needed a steady rhythm and a familiar form. So as soon as bands, even small bands, began to play the blues, they began to codify, to formalize the music's structure and to regularize its beat. Early jazz musicians found it easier to improvise on pieces that were simpler than the multi-strained rags, which left open the question, "Which strain do we improvise on?" Besides, the blues had an active improvisational tradition. Hence the gradual shift during the 1920's away from more complicated structures and hence the popularity of the blues as a jazz vehicle.

EARLY BANDS

That the earliest jazz bands played the blues seems clear. It may even be their ability to play the blues that defined them in people's minds as jazz bands, as opposed to merely brass bands which could play ragtime. Born in 1877, New Orleans cornetist Buddy Bolden formed a band around 1895. His contemporaries and those who came after him called it the first jazz band. Bolden probably could read music passably—there are conflicting opinions on that—but he was known for his blues playing. Another New Orleans cornetist, Peter Bocage, recalled in 1959: "He had a good tone, but didn't know what he was doing, couldn't read. He played everything in B^b. He played a lot of blues, slow drag, not too many fast numbers . . . Blues was their standby, slow blues" (Donald Marquis, *In Search of Buddy Bolden, First Man of Jazz*, p. 105). Bassist Pops Foster recalled in his autobiography that Bolden "played very good for the style of stuff

The Onward Brass Band of the 1960's and 1970's. For a photo of the original Onward group, see Chapter 3. (Courtesy Rutgers Institute of Jazz Studies)

he was doing. He played nothing but the blues and all that stink music, and he played it very loud" (*The Autobiography of Pops Foster, New Orleans Jazzman,* as told to Tom Stoddard, p. 16).

The obvious ambivalence with which the more accomplished young musician Foster talked of Bolden's rough style of playing is typical of the reaction of many New Orleans musicians, black and Creole, to the beginnings of jazz. The ambivalence is typical even of some of the trained musicians who were Buddy Bolden's contemporaries. To musicians who were trained to play in brass bands and in dance orchestras, this new style, particularly when it was played by less literate musicians, seemed coarse and undisciplined. By the time jazz and the blues were being played, the black brass bands had a long tradition of their own. Many were started during Reconstruction. Throughout the country at that time, there was a kind of boom in bands, and their popularity was such that they became in some instances, John Philip Sousa's band being the most obvious example, big business. Bands travelled around the country and abroad and played marches, rags, dance tunes, light classics and novelty numbers to large crowds.

The brass bands preceded jazz bands, and probably learned jazz from smaller, rougher bands like Bolden's or trumpeter Chris Kelly's, or from small "string bands," bands with prominent violin, guitar and string bass. Tom Bethell, in his book on New Orleans clarinetist George Lewis, speculates that "the brass bands of New Orleans gradually adopted the jazz idiom then emerging in New Orleans, which reverses the more normal belief that street music was a major influence on the development of jazz style" (Bethell, *George Lewis,*

p. 71). But band music was an influence on jazz style, if we can trust the early records, and in ways that have not been fully explored. Brass bands and string orchestras in New Orleans and elsewhere played stock arrangements of marches and other pieces, including rags. In a recent study of stock ragtime orchestrations, Thornton Hagert has noted a suggestive shift that took place between 1900 and 1910 in the way music was typically being arranged (Hagert, "Band and Orchestral Ragtime," in Hasse, *op. cit.*). Orchestrators around 1900 accounted for the possibility that their arrangements might be played by groups of any size by doubling the important parts. They might assign the job of playing the basic rhythm to as many as nine instruments, including bass drum, cello and trombone. Hagert says that an 1899 orchestration called "A Warm Reception" assigned the melody to violin and clarinet with the flute an octave above. The trombone played an upper bass part, the cornet at times doubled the melody, and the snare drum imitated the rhythms of the melody.

By 1910, Hagert observes, "the cornet was increasingly the primary wind instrument playing melody, and the clarinet was more and more relegated to a role of playing upper harmony parts and piccolo-like elaborations." The trombone began to play extended lines in harmony, becoming "another voice rather than mere accompaniment" and, "it was often featured prominently, playing humorous sliding solo passages, or harmonies and connective passages." As a first melody instrument, the violin was now competing with "the powerful cornet" and, as an upper harmony instrument, with the clarinet. It is significant that these changes in writing occur just when jazz was developing, and that they virtually describe the wind parts on the first jazz recordings of a few years later.

Around the turn of the century, drumming was being transformed as well. Several persons patented foot pedals for the bass drum: Dee Dee Chandler of New Orleans invented his in 1904 or 1905. Foot pedals allowed a single drummer to perform on several drums at once and to sit while doing so. (Hi-hat foot pedals came later, at the end of the 1920's.) Around the same time, new stands for the snare drum and cymbals added to the capabilities of the solo drummer. The development of the modern drumset was crucial to the future of jazz.

3 New Orleans

*"But the old-time musicians,
they didn't play nothing but music."*
—Peter Bocage (*In Search of Buddy Bolden*, p. 104)

In words that bring to mind Ferdinand in Shakespeare's *The Tempest* trying to locate the source of Ariel's singing, guitarist Danny Barker (b. 1909) spoke of the New Orleans of his youth: "One of my pleasantest memories as a kid growing up in New Orleans was how a bunch of us kids, playing, would suddenly hear sounds. It was like a phenomenon, like the Aurora Borealis—maybe. The sounds of men playing would be so clear, but we wouldn't be sure where they were coming from. So we'd start trotting, start running—'It's this way!' 'It's that way!'—And, sometimes, after running for a while, you'd find you'd be nowhere near that music. But that music could come on you any time like that. The city was full of the sounds of music" (*Hear Me Talkin' To Ya*, p. 3).

Barker was probably hearing one of the many brass bands that flourished in New Orleans, with their wide repertoire of marches and other musics. But what he described—a city full of the sounds of music—has been noted by almost every New Orleans musician who lived in the city in the first decades of the twentieth century. The ready availability of music of all kinds, from blues to opera, and the status accorded by black youths to true "musicianers," as Sidney Bechet called them, helps to explain the unique qualities of the music developed there.

It is undeniable that ragtime was being played and partially improvised elsewhere, and the blues was gradually spreading out of the South, and as a result something like jazz probably developed in other cities. Yet it seems equally undeniable that the music we think of today as jazz was initially a product of New Orleans and its environs. James P. Johnson said that although New York's pianists were exceptionally advanced before 1914, "There weren't any jazz bands like they had in New Orleans or on the Mississippi river boats" (Johnson, quoted in Hasse, p. 170). The major impact musicians like trumpeters Freddie Keppard and King Oliver, pianist Jelly Roll Morton, clarinetist Sidney

Bechet and especially Louis Armstrong had on Chicago's black population and on musicians both black and white is evidence that these men—all New Orleans products—brought something new from their hometown, something in addition to their enormous personal talents. Chris Goddard's study of early recordings by black musicians led him to conclude that "most black musicians, particularly those not from New Orleans, were not playing jazz before 1920" and that "the fact that such men had almost as much difficulty as whites in acquiring the new jazz skills is a powerful indication of the importance of New Orleans as the source of the music" (Chris Goddard, *Jazz Away From Home*, p. 27). Jazz was still new enough in 1920 that few musicians could play it. Lawrence Gushee's research on birthdates of early New Orleans players suggests that in fact writers may traditionally have placed the birth of jazz a little too early, at the 1890's or even 1900. Most players we know of were born around 1890, making it unlikely that any jazz as we know it was played before these people were in their teens, a little before 1910.

From his work on early recordings, Gushee has suggested some crucial differences between the earliest rags and jazz recorded by New Orleans musicians and that of New Yorkers. "New Orleans music is slower and more relaxed, due not so much to the fragrant breezes of the Mississippi delta as to the lesser impact of fast ragtime and one-step playing, the longer lives of some of the older dances (quadrilles, lancers, medium-tempo waltzes), and the greater influence of vocal blues and slow dancing of the rougher sort than in New York." And he summarizes, "We hear New York bands as assemblages of often very different musical personalities; we hear New Orleans bands, black or white, as units" (Notes to *Steppin' on the Gas: Rags to Jazz*, 1913–27, New World Records 269).

New Orleans was a unique city, particularly for blacks, some of whom, even before the Civil War, enjoyed certain freedoms there unavailable in the rest of the South. In 1900 the twelfth largest city in the country, New Orleans was a multi-racial, multi-ethnic city which still reflected the cultures of its Spanish, French, German, and African settlers. Although these groups mixed to a certain extent, a caste system remained, as Eileen Southern has pointed out (*The Music of Black Americans: A History*, p. 132). Before the Civil War, the city distinguished free whites (Americans, Creoles, German, Irish), "free colored" (some with French blood), and slaves. The black population grew rapidly in the latter part of the nineteenth century (20.5 percent between 1890 and 1900) until in 1900, blacks constituted a quarter of the population. Many of these new inhabitants came from the country, and they brought with them a taste for their folk musics and blues. Besides the relatively poor masses of black residents, New Orleans contained the "free colored," "a small, tight-knit, mainly French-speaking Negro elite with its own social clubs, debutantes, and business and professional men, some of whom even studied in France" (Joy Jackson, *New Orleans in the Gilded Age*, p. 19).

This elite had, among other things, a remarkable musical history in a city noted for its music: New Orleans had at one time in the nineteenth century three opera companies, and such early jazz artists as Sidney Bechet and Jelly Roll Morton remembered hearing opera. Southern reveals that in the 1830's a hundred member "Negro Philharmonic Society" was organized to present concerts. This kind of activity had a significant, though indirect, effect on many early jazzmen, because they were often tutored by musicians trained in the classics as well as in popular music.

More directly important to jazz were the brass bands and dance bands that were so popular among both black and white New Orleanians. In his *Brass Bands and New Orleans Jazz*, William Schafer asserts that "brass bands gave jazz its instrumentation, its instrumental techniques, its basic repertoire," but they were not, at least at first, jazz bands. Schafer agrees with Tom Bethell, cited in Chapter 2, that brass bands may have picked up jazz playing from dance bands after the new music became locally popular. Before that, brass bands read the marches, rags and popular pieces that they performed. "Only at the turn of the century, as the music we now call jazz began to be amalgamated by nonreading musicians, did brass bands incorporate much head [unwritten] music into their repertoires. Only slowly did they shift from reading standard printed band arrangements to developing improvisational, head arrangements" (p. 24).

It has been said that the end of the Civil War, during which many military groups were disbanded, resulted in a plethora of cheap brass instruments, many of which were bought by black musicians. We have seen no actual evidence for this claim, and the research of John Chilton suggests that, on the contrary, musicians probably hung onto their old instruments and that black musicians acquired instruments in the ways others did: from stores and from friends and family members. The instruments that were played in brass bands, and in early jazz, were not exactly the same that we use today. For example, the cornet was much more common than its now famous relative, the trumpet. (Cornets were common in several keys, whereas only the B^b trumpet is used in jazz today.) Most of the early brass "kings" were cornet players until the late twenties.

There is a common stereotype that only tubas and banjos were used in early jazz. As one can see in photographs, both tubas and string basses were used. (See, for example, the photographs on pp. 38, 50.) Many bassists could play either instrument depending on the situation—the louder tuba was useful at outdoor events, or when the band marched or recorded. Similarly, banjo players also tended to play guitar, using the banjo in situations when they needed to project more sound. Saxophones were used in brass bands and in early jazz, but were usually considered, until the 1920's, as just another instrument for the clarinetists to play. Clarinets were available in various types. The older Albert system clarinets were favored among New Orleans clarinetists, whereas modern musicians use the newer, and more convenient, Boehm clarinets. (The difference is in the way the keys were arranged—some clarinetists stuck to the more awkward Albert system because they believed they could get a richer sound than they could with the more fluent Boehm arrangement, with its added keys.) Clarinets, like cornets, also appeared in several keys, while today the B^b is standard.

In New Orleans, brass bands seemed omnipresent among blacks and whites. As Schafer has written, "In the years before 1900 a solid tradition of both self-trained provincial bands and municipal bands of skilled musicians was firmly established in the rich musical milieu around New Orleans" (p. 30). The provincial bands often had some training from visiting city professionals. These bands, often associated with mens' clubs and lodges, performed regularly on a variety of occasions: the brass bands could be found winding through the city's streets during Mardi Gras, but also promoting such diverse attractions as picnics and the campaign stops of local politicians. Brass bands and dance bands played regularly in the parks on the outskirts of New Orleans and on Lake Pontchartrain. Born in 1892, bassist Pops Foster moved to New Orleans with his family in 1902 and remembered spending Sunday afternoons in Lincoln Park. Lincoln Park was then an amusement park whose attractions included merry-go-rounds, roulette wheels, a hot air balloon—and bands. As Foster recalled, a brass band would play in the pavilion from four to five-thirty, and then from six to eight, John Robichaux's dance band would take over, to be replaced then by another brass band. The Robichaux band was photographed in 1896—its instrumentation was two violins, clarinet, two cornets, trombone, string bass and drums. The drummer, Dee Dee Chandler, is pictured behind a bass drum: this was before he designed the foot pedal mentioned at the end of Chapter 2. (The photo is in Rose and Souchon, *New Orleans Jazz*, p. 180.) In his teens, Foster remembers finding 35 to 40 bands playing at Lake Pontchartrain and at Milneberg Park (*The Autobiography of Pops Foster, New Orleans Jazzman*, pp. 13–16).

Whereas a dance band such as John Robichaux's, with fiddles and a string bass, played for dances and parties, the brass bands played for funerals and marches as well. At a funeral they would march slowly towards the burying ground to the sound of dirges and a muffled drum. After the burial, the band, picking up the tempo at the signal of the snare drummer or of the lead cornet, and accompanied by dancing on the sidelines (by children and onlookers known as the second line), would play a joyous up-tempo piece on the way back to town: "Oh, Didn't He Ramble" was a favorite according to Louis Armstrong and others.

This tradition is not merely a black folkway, nor was it confined to the South. The earliest known reference to such a funeral in this country comes from poet Walt Whitman, who in 1829 observed a funeral for some white sailors killed in an explosion in Brooklyn: "It was a full military and naval funeral—the sailors marching two by two, hand in hand, banners tied up and bound in black crepe, the muffled drums beating, the bugles wailing for the mournful peals of a dead march . . . We remember the soldiers firing the salute over the grave. And then how everything changed with the dashing and merry jig played by the same bugles and drums, as they made their exit from the graveyard and wended rapidly home" (Justin Kaplan, *Walt Whitman: A Life*, p. 68). What distinguished the blacks using this tradition was, of course, their choice of music and the manner in which they performed it.

The brass bands would have had up to 12 members each: certainly few were much larger. They would play "for circuses, carnivals, minstrel and medicine shows, political rallies, churches, picnics, dances, athletic contests, holiday

The original Onward Brass Band, about 1913. Fourth from left is Lorenzo Tio, Jr., teacher of many famous clarinetists. (Courtesy Rutgers Institute of Jazz Studies)

gatherings," as well as funerals, according to Schafer (p. 8). They maintained proudly their tradition of "careful reading and execution [of] 'legitimate' brass band music, until somewhere around the turn of the century when ragtime brass bands began to appear. Then 'ear' musicians, 'routiners' who made up head arrangements of simple tunes, began to dominate black brass bands of New Orleans" (Schafer, p. 32). (A memorized head arrangement was a "routine": hence the name "routiners.").

What accounted for the gradual invasion of the traditional brass band, with its proud, reading musicians, by a looser, less scholarly style? For one thing, there was the worsening racial situation in New Orleans, culminating in the so-called Robert Charles race riot of 1900. In 1894, an amendment to the so-called Black Code stated that anyone of African descent, including the Creoles of color, would henceforth be considered black. One result was that Creole musicians lost some of their jobs to white bands; another was that Creoles and blacks, musicians and non-musicians, would work together more frequently. One theory holds that jazz was the result of the mixing of trained Creole musicians, with their ability to play brass band and dance music, with the less trained black musicians, who brought to the Creoles their grounding in the blues. That meant that some of the trained musicians heard something they wanted to emulate in the rough playing of their black companions, and that some black musicians found ways of gaining more skill on their instruments and as readers. Of course not every Creole musician was a skillful reader: Sidney Bechet, for one, never learned to read music well. Nor did every young black musician pick up these skills at this time: Louis Armstrong at the time he left New Orleans was not yet a proficient reader.

The mixing of musicians also meant that a generation of reading musicians was forced into a position where it could be upstaged by less learned instrumentalists improvising or "routining," making up arrangements in a new style. Not surprisingly, some of the trained musicians resented the youngsters. Whatever one might think about the origin of jazz, New Orleans musicians repeatedly distinguish between the note-reading Creole musicians, who were supposed to live Downtown, and the black improvisers Uptown, who played a rough, bluesy kind of jazz: "ratty," the Creoles called it. The comments of fiddler Paul Dominguez, quoted in *Mister Jelly Roll* (p. 75), are typical: "You know what happen to us musicians—I mean us real musicians from the Seventh Ward where we were all educated in music and *knew* our instruments—when we came in here, we had to change. Why, my daddy, he was recognized king bass player in this town, but he wouldn't play *ratty*. He wouldn't play unless you put his part up in front of him, and then he could make a monkey out of the average player of today."

One can see bass players like Dominguez's father in photographs of early New Orleans dance bands, which show violins, guitars, and string basses beside the clarinets, trumpets, trombones and occasional saxophones. The string bassist would often use a bow, even while keeping a beat. These often informally organized "string bands" are even less well documented than the brass bands, which survived to record in the 1940's.

Because the pre-jazz dance bands and orchestras went unrecorded, we cannot judge, or even describe precisely, their music, except that their repertoire at the turn of the century included waltzes, quadrilles, and arrangements of popular songs, as well as, in some cases, rags and blues. They almost certainly played an important part in the early history of jazz. It is likely that an improvisatory, "ratty" style based on blues and loose arrangements of material previously played in earlier styles, began to infiltrate established groups gradually around the turn of the century. Even white groups were affected. A white band leader, Papa Jack Laine, claimed that his groups, which were tutored by two black musicians, Achille Bacquet and Dave Perkins, were "ragging" tunes, improvising on them, as early as 1885 (*In Search of Buddy Bolden*, p. 34). It is of course possible that Laine, something of a braggart, was wrong about the date, but it is important to note that blacks and whites interacted from the start.

The groups we have been describing only rarely included a piano. Though the piano now seems an inevitable part of a dance band, judging from the photographs of early New Orleans bands, it did not seem so inevitable in the early part of the century. Pianos of course could not be used outdoors, where many of the jobs for these all-purpose bands were found. Nonetheless, pianists did have an impact on early jazz. They were, after all, usually the most carefully trained instrumentalists, and in the groups in which they did appear, they were frequently called upon to be the arranger and musical director. But for the most part in New Orleans at the turn of the century, they typically played as soloists or with small groups in bars and even brothels, which gave rise to the disproven theory that jazz was born in these disreputable—but in New Orleans at least— often quite elegant, surroundings.

BUDDY BOLDEN

The first jazz band, according to musicians and scholars and legend, was led by black cornetist Buddy Bolden, whose life and work has been documented by Donald Marquis (*In Search of Buddy Bolden, First Man of Jazz*). Bolden was born in an integrated neighborhood of New Orleans in 1877. As a boy, he must have heard examples of all the music we have been discussing, and he attended St. John the Fourth Baptist Church on First Street, where he heard vigorous renditions of spirituals and hymns. By 1895 he was playing cornet regularly. According to Marquis, he probably played as a sideman in parades. He "developed his style in the small string bands playing for dances and parties" (Marquis, p. 42). "His efforts took the form of playing 'wide-open' on the cornet and of playing in up-tempo or ragging the hymns, street songs, and dance tunes to create a musical sound that people were unfamiliar with" (Marquis, p. 43). However, Lawrence Gushee, a leading researcher of early jazz, doubts that hymns would have been played at that time anywhere but at funerals. Hymn playing by jazz groups may have come in with the New Orleans jazz revival of the forties–and those groups may have been influenced by the success of recordings such as Louis Armstrong's 1938 "When the Saints Come Marching In."

Bolden would embroider the melodies he played, and emphasize their rhythm. As Wallace Collins told it, "He'd take one note [of the original] and put two or three to it" (Martin Williams, *Jazz Masters of New Orleans*, p. 1). Presumably he was gradually loosening up the rhythms that marked marches, ragtime, and later, many of the popular songs of the new century. By 1900, Bolden was a full-time professional musician and until he was affected by the mental illness that resulted in his being incarcerated in 1907, he was "King Bolden" in New Orleans. Bolden is best remembered for his sheer lungpower–you could hear him miles away, according to legend–and for his blues. Creole clarinetist George Bacquet heard Bolden at the Odd Fellows Hall, and spoke of it in 1940: "I'd never heard anything like that before. I'd played 'legitimate' stuff. But this, it was something that pulled me in. They got me on the stand and I played with them. After that I didn't play legitimate so much" (*Down Beat*, Dec. 15, 1940). Trombone player Bill Matthews said, "On those old, slow, low down blues, he had a moan in his cornet that went all through you, just like you were in church or something" (Marquis, p. 100).

Bolden's main rival from 1900 until the premature end of his career was not another ragging band, but the straighter John Robichaux Orchestra. Other bands included the Olympia Brass Band, started by cornetist Freddie Keppard, who has the distinction of having had the chance, which he declined, to be the first jazzman to record; the Superior Jazz Band, with cornetist Bunk Johnson, who would spark the New Orleans revival of the 1940's; the Peerless and Onward Brass Bands and various groups with cornetist Manuel Perez and, after 1908, Joe Oliver.

New Orleans music began to spread by the second decade of the century. As early as 1908, Freddie Keppard took his band on tour. Pianist Tony Jackson, a favorite of Jelly Roll Morton, was in Chicago by 1911. The Creole Band, a famous early group that regrettably never recorded, was founded in Los Angeles in 1914, where it appeared, and was written about, at a heavyweight prize fight. It was in Chicago in 1915. In the middle of a peripatetic early career in vaudeville, Jelly Roll Morton made it to Chicago for the first time in 1910. He also resided in St. Louis and parts of Texas. Other early jazz musicians travelled as well. Bassist Pops Foster claimed: "New Orleans bands had been travelling since way early. I remember around 1914 or 1915 I played Dallas, Texas with the Original Tuxedo Band" (*The Autobiography of Pops Foster*, p. 128).

Black music was being carried up the river in the teens and later, as New Orleans bands were hired to entertain on the steamboats: Louis Armstrong first left his home in 1919 with the Fate Marable band that worked on the Streckfus line. In 1917, the military order was given that helped speed this dispersal, though it did not, as often claimed, cause it: the closing, by the order of the Navy, of New Orleans' red light district, Storyville. While few bands worked the brothels that made this district infamous—and theoretically dangerous to the war effort—Storyville had provided jobs for some pianists and, in the outlying bars, for some dance groups as well. These players had to look elsewhere for work.

4 The Early Recordings

The burgeoning recording industry would have a crucial effect on black music. Black ragtime and dance band recordings began to appear that had elements of what was later called jazz. James Reese Europe (1881–1919) was a black orchestra leader who started his career conducting travelling shows. Through the teens he conducted his large "Society Orchestra," which, among other things, backed up the white dance team of Irene and Vernon Castle from 1914 to 1917. Then, during the First World War, Europe, now a lieutenant and leader of the 369th Infantry Regiment Band, toured the continent. The earlier band recorded a heavy-sounding group of ragtime pieces, including "Castle House Rag" of 1914. The arrangement is made ponderous, despite its shrill, somewhat rushed first strain, by the excessive use of unison playing. There is little improvisation in this recording, which is notable mainly for the vigorous, enlivening drumming of Buddy Gilmore in the last choruses. In contrast, recordings by the saxophone band called the Six Brown Brothers, a white group—not all brothers—show them playing a very literal kind of ragtime. Their "Down Home Rag" of 1915 is almost classical in style. (Both recordings can be found on the invaluable collection *Steppin' on the Gas*, New World Records 269.)

Another bandleader who worked with ragtime is the famous W.C. Handy, earlier mentioned as the composer of "St. Louis Blues," "Memphis Blues," and many others. Handy, who was born in Alabama in 1873 and died in 1958, worked with a minstrel show around the turn of the century, then began touring with his own band before settling in New York and founding a publishing and recording company. His working groups were sometimes large ragtime orchestras that in 1917 recorded such numbers as "Livery Stable Blues" and his version of "Maple Leaf Rag"—the "Fuzzy Wuzzy Rag." This recording, with its violins and xylophone added to a more standard "jazz" instrumentation, contains no

James Reese Europe around 1914. (Courtesy Rutgers Institute of Jazz Studies)

improvisation. But it does have passages in which the trombones swoop in the style of the day.

These and other recordings show that ragtime and blues were expanding and developing a wider audience. More importantly, they suggest the way the new music, jazz, was developing. The distinction between ragtime and jazz was ready to be made. According to New Orleans pianist and composer Jelly Roll Morton, ragtime, like the blues, was a form of music and, he implied, a specific repertoire of pieces. He said that jazz, on the other hand, was an *approach* to music that can be applied to any piece. He deserves to be quoted in full: "Ragtime is a certain type of syncopation and only certain tunes can be played in that idea. But jazz is a style that can be applied to any type of tune" (Alan Lomax, *Mister Jelly Roll* p. 62). Morton claimed that he was creating jazz, that he was "jazzing" tunes and calling the music jazz, since 1902, an unlikely date since it is now known that he was born in 1890. But jazz itself did not become a national—and international—force until it was first recorded in 1917. Ironically,

W.C. Handy on the Ed Sullivan television show, late 1950's. (Courtesy Rutgers Institute of Jazz Studies)

those recordings were made by a white group, whose leader later asserted that *he* invented jazz. The group was called the Original Dixieland Jazz Band, and they helped make "jazz" a household word.

THE ODJB AND OTHER NEW ORLEANS BANDS

The group that, after several personnel changes, would become the Original Dixieland Jazz Band took its first step towards fame on March 2, 1916, when drummer Johnny Stein, clarinetist Alcide Nuñez, trombonist Eddie Edwards, and cornetist Nick La Rocca left New Orleans for Chicago, opening the next day at Schiller's Cafe on East 31st Street. They were not the first white jazz band to play at Schiller's: Tom Brown led a group there in 1915. But they were startlingly successful. Originally led by drummer Stein, the band played bright, nervy versions of New Orleans numbers such as "High Society" and "Tiger Rag." They received their first press, in the *Chicago Herald*, on May 1, 1916, when a columnist decried the "singing, shouting" and "drunken laughter" that attended what was then called "Stein's Dixie Jass Band." A month later, in a coup of sorts, Stein was ousted from the band and replaced by Tony Sbarbaro (also known as Spargo); on October 31, clarinetist Nuñez was replaced by Larry Shields.

The following January 27, they were in Manhattan, playing at Reisen-weber's Restaurant, and being advertised as "The First Sensational Amusement Novelty of 1917." Three days later they recorded two pieces, in two takes each, that were rejected by Columbia Records, only to be issued after the band had proved a hit. (Each recording of a piece is a *take*, and usually only one take is released for sale.) On February 26, still billed as the "Original Dixieland Jass Band," they recorded "Livery Stable Blues" and "Dixie[land] Jass Band One Step" for Victor Records. Released on March 7, these records made history, selling at least 250,000 copies (Victor asserted that they sold a million).

These recordings, and the ones that followed by the Original Dixieland Jazz Band—they adopted the spelling "jazz" by the time of their second recording session—have received throughout the years little respect from critics and historians. Although we too regret that superior black bands were not recorded at that time, the ODJB sides are not only historically important, but artistically respectable. They continued to influence Dixieland groups worldwide for decades to come. Every such group plays "Tiger Rag," "At the Jazz Band Ball," "Fidgety Feet," and the "Royal Garden Blues," all introduced by the ODJB. For several years, their 78's were the only jazz recordings available, and when they travelled in 1919 to Europe, they introduced live jazz to the continent and England. Soon, there were recordings of the ODJB repertoire by bands in Germany, England and France.

They were billed as a novelty group, and their recordings are full of shrill clarinet shrieks, comical trombone swoops, and other ostensibly amusing sound effects. "Livery Stable Blues" begins with a competent ensemble chorus at mid-tempo. Insistently accented, it gets its name from its carefully planned breaks, in which one hears first clarinetist Shields crow and then cornetist La Rocca whinny, followed by a slowly ascending glissando by trombonist Edwards. It soon becomes obvious that the band was not improvising as do modern jazz

The Original Dixieland Jazz Band, 1916. From left to right: Tony Sbarbaro (aka Spargo), Eddie Edwards, Nick LaRocca, Alcide Nuñez (who was replaced by Larry Shields), Henry Ragas. (Courtesy Rutgers Institute of Jazz Studies)

bands: Each subsequent chorus virtually repeats the music that has already been played.

The ODJB's jittery version of "Tiger Rag," recorded with little variation in 1917, 1918, and again in 1919, was based on a piece New Orleans musicians simply called "Number Two." There was no single composer: The music was still part of an aural tradition. It became the most recorded jazz piece in the world through 1942, as can be seen in Brian Rust's standard discography, with Handy's "St. Louis Blues" a close second. The most famous of its themes is the last, which has the trombone doing a "tiger" growl while sliding and the band answering musically what is known as "Hold that tiger!" (or "Where's that tiger?"). (See music example.)

Example 4–1.
"Tiger Rag," third theme.

In the ODJB's "Tiger Rag" we hear more clearly the clipped cornet style of La Rocca (b. 1889). La Rocca's playing derives from marching band cornet, and it resembles that of a black contemporary, Freddie Keppard. The excitement of the piece—and of many of the ODJB's recordings—derives from its fast tempo and from the barely audible but dynamic percussion work of Tony Spargo. Larry Shields, on tunes such as "Clarinet Marmalade," seems to be the most competent wind player. The band had a lasting impact, fixing in the minds of a wide audience an image of jazz as a jivey, uptempo music that was, as a prosy poster advertising the ODJB's appearance at the Palladium in London said, the "last word of a gee whiz world."

The ODJB itself did not last. They based their appeal on novelty, and yet they were unable to renew themselves. Until they disbanded at the beginning of 1925, they imitated their first recordings, rerecording their earlier hits, such as "Tiger Rag," with few changes. They never equalled their first records and were eclipsed in popularity by their own imitators.

Meanwhile, record companies sought more groups in the ODJB vein. Another important group of white musicians, The Louisiana Five, was led by a clarinetist whom the ODJB had fired: Alcide Nuñez. In December 1918, The Louisiana Five recorded three sides, using Nuñez's clarinet as lead and dispensing with a cornet. The band introduced "A Good Man is Hard to Find," a song which became immediately popular among jazz bands. (It's an indication of how fast the music was travelling in those days that "A Good Man is Hard to Find" was recorded by a British group, the Savoy Quartet, as early as September 1919.) The Louisiana Five's most satisfying number, "Church Street Sobbin' Blues," was recorded in March, 1919.

The same month, another group, the Original New Orleans Jazz Band, recorded its third session. (Its first was in November 1918.) Another imitation of the ODJB, this band had two main distinctions. It waxed for the first time the lasting Dixieland classic, "Ja Da," and its pianist was Jimmy Durante, who became a star of Hollywood and television.

The New Orleans Rhythm Kings was a more distinctive band. At its heart were three New Orleans natives who were boyhood friends—cornetist Paul Mares, trombonist George Brunis, and clarinetist Leon Roppolo. They first recorded as the "Friar's Society Orchestra" in 1922, and then, with a different supporting cast, again in March 1923. At these sessions they introduced a variety of tunes that remain in the repertoire of Dixieland groups all over the world: "Farewell Blues," "Tin Roof Blues," "Panama" and "Bugle Call Blues," among them. The group is distinguished by Mares's sweet-sounding trumpet, in the same tradition as King Oliver, by clarinetist Roppolo's rounded tones and lyrical accompaniments, and by Brunis's relatively subtle trombone playing. Their light, lively swing on "Panama" distinguishes them from the frantic drive of the ODJB. Their humor—as in the wobbly clarinet break on "Bugle Call Blues"—is also less strained. Their pleasingly relaxed "Tin Roof Blues" demonstrates their skillful ensemble work and attractive solos. The N.O.R.K., as they are called, did one more remarkable thing: They had Jelly Roll Morton play piano for them at a session on July 17, 1923, thus making themselves the first integrated recording band.

New Orleans trombonist Kid Ory made the first recordings by a black jazz band. Born in La Place, Louisiana probably in 1886, Ory led a successful band in New Orleans from 1912 to 1919, developing at the same time the swooping style of trombone playing that he would carry with him to his death in 1971. With its long slides and brisk punctuation of the beat, Ory's playing came to be known as "tailgate trombone," after the New Orleans custom of transporting bands around the city to ballyhoo events—they would play facing the back of the truck, the open tailgate. Ory moved to Los Angeles in 1919, where he met up with New Orleans trumpeter Mutt Carey.

In 1922, they recorded two genial, low-key numbers: "Ory's Creole Trombone" and the multi-thematic "Society Blues." (These recordings were originally issued as being played by "Spikes' Seven Pods of Pepper Orchestra," despite the fact that the band was at most a sextet.) "Ory's Creole Trombone" is built around the repeated breaks by Ory, breaks which he renders with verve and bluster. It has a pleasant initial theme, and it is graced throughout by the unassuming cornet of Mutt Carey. Born in 1891, Carey plays with warm-toned charm and rhythmic liveliness. His phrases have none of the pointed, staccato jauntiness of Nick La Rocca's. As Lawrence Gushee has pointed out, these records are also notable for their avoidance of novelty instrumental effects.

It is now impossible to state definitively whether these records preserve a New Orleans style older than that which would be recorded in 1923, whether the gentle swing captured here demonstrates a quality of New Orleans jazz before it was adapted to the faster pace of Chicago nightlife, or whether, as

Gushee has suggested, the easy bounce of "Society Blues" is rather a result of the incomplete rhythm section. (They have no banjo player, and the string bass, listed as played by Ed Garland, is inaudible.) The Ory selections share an easy rhythmic flow with the recordings made by people like New Orleans cornetist Bunk Johnson—a predecessor of Armstrong—during the New Orleans revival of the forties. Ory's recordings seem linked stylistically to the work of a near contemporary of Mutt Carey, Freddie Keppard, who was born in 1890.

Keppard, who was not recorded until 1924, played in various New Orleans bands in his teens. He travelled to Los Angeles early in 1914 to work with the Creole Orchestra organized by bassist Bill Johnson. He went to Chicago and New York with the band in 1915. He spent most of the rest of his life working in Chicago, where he died almost forgotten in 1933.

His best recordings, such as "Messin' Around," were made in 1926: they show him to be a considerable blues player and a pleasant melodist, with a clipped style that is appealingly varied. Recorded with a group dubbed Cookie's Gingersnaps, "Messin' Around" begins with a bit of vaudeville talk, common in twenties recordings; then the band plays the 16-bar verse. Keppard enters with an expressive, smearing solo statement that initially sticks close to the simple melody. His playing on the following chorus is notable for its bounce, for its shadings of vibrato and sound and for its subtle variations of rhythm. (A different tune entitled "Messin' Around," recorded in 1926 by Jimmy Blythe, is also said to feature Keppard, but Gushee suspects it is a different cornetist.)

Those carefully controlled sounds are what give the marvelous vocal quality to Keppard's statements on "Salty Dog," whose two takes were recorded in September 1926 for Paramount Records. And it is the evidence of that control that makes the oft-written stories of Keppard's supposed decrepitude at the time of those sessions seem doubtful. Usually told by persons who want to build a reputation for Keppard to rival Armstrong's, these tales of Keppard's former prowess have little supporting evidence. Keppard may have been a stronger player earlier, but there is nothing to suggest that he was a more advanced one. His choruses on "Salty Dog" and elsewhere demonstrate a fine bluesy talent expressed in a style that Armstrong would eclipse.

NEW YORK PERFORMERS

For the most part, we have been talking about groups with ties to New Orleans. New York was even in the twenties the center of the music business in America, and Harlem a large black community with its own stars. A New York recording session of August 10, 1920 proved of crucial historical importance to jazz, perhaps opening the way for some of the recording sessions already discussed. That was when Mamie Smith, a vaudeville and sometime blues singer, recorded "Crazy Blues," the first blues by a black singer, initiating a fad for the blues that would bring to the fore such greater singers as Gertrude "Ma" Rainey and Bessie and Clara Smith. Born in Cincinnati in 1883, Mamie Smith left home—probably when she was ten—as a dancer, and in her teens, she danced with Tutt-Whitney's Smart Set Company and began to sing. A vivacious personality, she started around 1913 to work in nightclubs and theaters around New York. In 1918, she appeared in Perry Bradford's musical revue, "Maid of Harlem." Her hit song in that revue was "Harlem Blues."

Bradford too was a show business veteran: he was also a determined musician and entrepreneur. (His nickname was Mule.) He observed the success of Mamie Smith's singing with the Harlem crowd, and decided to record her. He had little luck at first. Record companies were unconvinced that a black blues singer could be a commercial success. In January 1920, Victor rejected a test record by Smith. OKeh Records was interested in Bradford's songs, though. In February 1920, Bradford had Mamie Smith record "That Thing Called Love" and "You Can't Keep a Good Man Down." (This latter record became part of a wave of songs suggesting what could or could not be done with a good man: Other songs questioned whether such a creature existed.) OKeh put out the record, billing the singer as "Mamie Smith, contralto."

It sold well. Next Bradford wanted to record his "Harlem Blues." OKeh wanted the rotund white vaudeville singer Sophie Tucker to belt it out. Tucker was unavailable, so Mamie Smith recorded the tune, renamed as "Crazy Blues," and, on the other side, the amusing "It's Right Here For You." To everyone's surprise, the record was a hit, selling 75,000 copies in a month in Harlem alone. Today, Smith's belting style and her stiff accompaniment sound dated. But it

Mamie Smith and her band, 1920. At the piano is Willie "the Lion" Smith. (Courtesy Rutgers Institute of Jazz Studies)

was the first such blues on record, and Smith's fans loved it. The sales of "Crazy Blues" and other of her records encouraged record companies to search for other blues singers and jazz players, and to record them for what would be called "race" records, labels designed specifically for blacks. Destructive though this policy of segregated record offerings may have been for the wider reputation of black musicians, it did ensure that an increasingly broad spectrum of those performers were recorded.

In many of her recordings Mamie Smith was accompanied by a New York jazz star, trumpeter Johnny Dunn. Born in 1897, Dunn had played with W.C. Handy's band in his hometown, Memphis. He was in New York by 1920, fast becoming "one of the biggest names in the Negro entertainment world throughout most of the twenties" (Charters and Kunstadt, *Jazz: A History of the New York Scene,* p. 86). At the beginning of the twenties, he was New York's top jazz trumpeter, known for his tricks with mutes—he probably played the first plunger solo on record—and for his blues. Dunn soloed with even eighth notes, and he relied on staccato articulation. His "Bugle Blues," recorded in December 1921, finds him playing with a rackety large group, and soloing discreetly. It was an influential hit. His plunger solos are said to have influenced Bubber Miley, who would make the plunger sound a crucial part of Duke Ellington's style.

Dunn made some important sides in 1928 in a session with Jelly Roll Morton on piano, sides in which his piercing sound is placed in a well organized context. Dunn opens the second chorus with a "vo-do-de-o" motive also found in the playing of Oliver and others. (See music example.) Later he solos with the plunger mute, to greater effect. His rhythms are generally square, but in the climactic ensemble of this piece he creates a strong dragging effect by slowing down to quarter-note triplets. Equally notable are some of the band's effects: the creative cymbal work behind Dunn's first unmuted solo, the fast alto sax runs after this cymbal work, and the wild tuba playing at the end. But Dunn's star fell with the rise of Louis Armstrong, who was to be the next trumpet sensation.

Example 4—2
Johnny Dunn, first phrase of his solo on "Sergeant Dunn's Bugle Call Blues.

JELLY ROLL MORTON

In 1923, despite the music's New Orleans roots, and New York's economic power, Chicago was the key city in the jazz world. The black ghetto of the South Side, with its clubs and dance halls such as the Lincoln Gardens, the Dreamland, the Pekin and Sunset Cafes, was its key neighborhood. Many of these places were run by gangsters. The memories of twenties' jazz musicians are filled with stories of mobsters who seemed to shed fifty dollar bills like fall leaves, of all night jam sessions and occasional gun battles that set the band scurrying behind the piano, and, more seriously, of considerable intimidation by their employers. Earl Hines remembered playing seven nights a week until four in the morning at the Sunset Cafe. Later he went to the Grand Terrace, and he told how that club was taken over by gangsters who walked in one night and demanded twenty-five percent of the income in return for what was laughably called protection. All this might have been uncomfortably familiar to New Orleans musicians: There was a serious gangster element in Storyville as well.

Among the New Orleans greats who had by 1923 settled into Chicago, with its active musical life, was Jelly Roll Morton, a pianist, composer and arranger who had been a gambler, poolshark, pimp, dancer and vaudevillian, and who would before his death in 1941 turn into what James Joyce called in another context "a praiser of his own past." That past was illustrious, and did not need to be embroidered. In the twenties, Morton was a crucial performer, a fine pianist and a composer who came up with innovative ways of organizing small band performances. The recordings his band made in 1926 remain illuminating for their graceful swing and clear conception, for their clever construction and variety.

Thanks to the scholarship of Lawrence Gushee, it is known that Morton was born Ferdinand Lamothe in New Orleans in 1890. (The spelling on census records, Lemott, was probably phonetic.) Later Morton would say that his family name was La Menthe—it sounded more impressively French—and that he was born in 1885. Morton was one of the few persons in show business to claim that he was older than he was. He probably did so to bolster his assertion that he invented jazz in 1902, a feat which could hardly have been possible to a twelve-year-old. (He also claimed he invented swing.) Many remember Morton as a loud-talking braggart, whose mouth was his own worst enemy. Yet few add that he was brought up in a world in which entertainers, and particularly piano ticklers, were supposed to be flamboyant, to wear the finest suits with the flashiest linings, in order to impress the ladies and the rest of the audience as well. Morton's extravagance should be seen in the context of a culture which saw its prime pianists as heroes. He wasn't the only pianist to have a hundred suits. In New York, James P. Johnson and Willie "the Lion" Smith—and later Duke Ellington—rivalled his wardrobe. Morton went one step further. In his prosperous years he wore, as Albert Murray described, "a diamond ring, a diamond horseshoe pin, a watch circled with diamonds, a diamond-studded gold belt buckle, and a huge half-carat diamond in one of his front teeth." Morton's vanity and loud-talking, though excessive, fit the culture in which he performed. They may also have been the first line of defense for a sensitive man in a tough world.

His pride meant that he demanded to be treated fairly. Trumpeter Lee Collins recorded with Morton in 1924. Before the recording session, Collins went with Morton to see the manager of a big South-Side ballroom. As Collins tells it, "He and this man could not come to any agreement on the price Jelly wanted for

playing there. He told the manager, 'You bring [white bandleader] Paul Whiteman out here and pay any price he wants because he has the name of 'King of
Jazz.' But you happen to be talking to the real king of jazz. I invented it and I
brought it here' " (*Oh, Didn't He Ramble: The Life Story of Lee Collins*, pp. 37–38).
At the time that seemed like hopeless effrontery; today it might be seen as
welcome self-assertion.

Morton had other characteristics as well. He was loyal to his family, and in
his last years when he was ill and seemingly forgotten, he proved touchingly
courageous and determined. Gunther Schuller has called Morton the music's
first great composer. He had a clear idea of what he wanted to hear, and he
created three-minute performances that vividly realized his conceptions. He was
an entertainer, a buoyant singer and enlivening pianist, and something of a wit.

Morton's early career—or careers—took place in and around New Orleans.
While in his teens he played briefly in New Orleans sporting houses. Presumably he was playing blues, ragtime, popular songs and rearranged light classics.
He worked his way into Mississippi and through Louisiana as a pianist and
pool-hustler, performing at times with a vaudeville troupe. He toured various
theaters with his first wife, Rosa. Gradually he began to work further and
further from home, visiting Texas, Kansas City and St. Louis and moving
temporarily to Chicago in 1914. On September 15, 1915, Morton's "Jelly Roll
Blues" was published, with instrumental parts, in Chicago by Will Rossiter. This
was probably the first published jazz arrangement: Its title page says that it was
arranged by pianist Mel Stitzel.

Morton played primarily on the West Coast from the end of 1917 until May
1923, when he settled in Chicago. The New Orleans Rhythm Kings session of
1923 mentioned above included two takes of Morton's "Mr. Jelly Lord," and his
"London Blues." On July 18, he recorded a solo version of "Grandpa's Spells," a
ragtime-influenced piece with three themes that he probably wrote much earlier,
according to authority James Dapogny. As arranged by Morton for his "Red Hot
Peppers," this zestful composition was recorded for Victor Records in 1926
(SCCJ).

Morton orchestrates "Grandpa's Spells" brilliantly. At the outset the solo
banjo is answered by the lively chords of the band. The last version of the
second theme features an unusual duet between trombone and walking bass. A
lively piano solo by Morton brings the piece to the final ensemble, girded by the
creative cymbal work of Andrew Hilaire, who with Johnny St. Cyr on banjo and
John Lindsay on bass, formed one of the liveliest rhythm sections of the
twenties.

The 1926 small group recordings have been highly regarded from the
beginning, although for varying reasons. Once thought of as the essence of
improvised New Orleans jazz, they are now recognized to be careful compositions and arrangements. A middle ground might be found: we admire Morton's
architectural powers, his ability to build and arrange coherent pieces with swift
and yet readily comprehensible textural changes, and yet we respond immediately to the graceful swing of the first choruses of "Dead Man Blues," which

Publicity pose of Jelly Roll Morton and his Red Hot Peppers, 1926. From left to right: Andrew Hilaire (drums), Kid Ory (trombone), George Mitchell, John Lindsay, Morton, Johnny St. Cyr, Omer Simeon. (Courtesy Rutgers Institute of Jazz Studies)

after an introduction that parodies a funeral procession, moves into an easy, joyous walking four. And we revel in the slow-moving grace of "Smoke House Blues" and the way the tense, jerky introductory phrases of "The Chant" yield to a pounding swing, a swing that becomes more intense in the stomping last choruses.

The emphasis on Morton's writing has led to an undervaluing of some of the marvelous small group sides he made over the years, including a trio version of "Mr. Jelly Lord" with clarinetist Johnny Dodds sounding zestfully confident in a way he rarely was with Louis Armstrong. For all his braggadocio, Morton must have been a good man to work with: Musicians such as clarinetist Omer Simeon have praised Morton's seriousness, and his clear directions. Morton knew exactly what he wanted from his musicians and they respected him enough to give it to him.

His reputation as a pianist has fluctuated wildly. When Morton came to New York in 1928, James P. Johnson and Duke Ellington thought he wasn't much, at least by Manhattan's stringent standards. It was partly a question of regional styles. Morton came out of a southern blues and stomp tradition. The New Yorkers were used to a suaver approach. Still, Morton's stomping piano solos are brilliant extensions of the ragtime tradition. His accompaniments are enlivening: They push soloists along vigorously without covering them up or intimidating them. (Listen to the way Morton introduces and then accompanies

Simeon on "Doctor Jazz.") He was a great entertainer, and an appealing vocalist who made up in spirit for what he lacked in voice. Morton's 1939 version of "Winin' Boy Blues," recorded for Victor's Bluebird label well after the height of his career, has the same zest and winning appeal as the "Doctor Jazz" he sang and played in 1926.

Morton's career declined in the thirties, as big bands in swing arrangements replaced the small groups he had pioneered. He made no recordings from the end of 1930 until mid-1938. But he was not forgotten. For one thing, he had written one of swing's most popular pieces, "King Porter Stomp," a forward-looking composition that Morton had composed, astonishingly, in 1906. Another three-theme piece, "King Porter Stomp" ends in a riffing third strain that virtually demands the intense call-and-response treatment given it in a big band version by Fletcher Henderson that was also recorded by Benny Goodman. Morton recorded it as a piano solo on July 17, 1923, and then in duet with cornetist King Oliver in December 1924. Among other recordings, a 1939 solo recording appears in SCCJ. The piece made quite an impact when played by a full band. But Morton, increasingly embittered during the thirties, held to ideals of jazz which he thought big band swing had abandoned: he believed in the importance of variety, of vigorous swing constrained by careful constructions. He didn't want to hear whole reed or trumpet sections playing the same phrases. Swing music seemed to him a gross simplification of his own music.

That Morton's final years were productive is largely credited to folklorist Alan Lomax, who over several weeks in 1938 recorded for the Library of Congress acetates of Morton talking marvelously about his own past and about the history of his music, and illustrating his talk with splendid piano playing. (These were later issued to the public.) In 1939 and 1940, Morton made records for two different labels. He died in Los Angeles in 1941, just as a revival of New Orleans music was getting underway. Over fifty years later, in 1992, his life was dramatized in a hit Broadway musical, *Jelly's Last Jam*.

"KING" JOE OLIVER

Morton's key recordings were made in 1926; Joe Oliver's were made even earlier, in a nine-month period beginning in April 1923. Oliver's last sides came only eight years later. Morton did not flourish in the swing era, but Oliver disappeared during it, and yet Oliver was perhaps even more influential in the early years of jazz. His band, with the young Louis Armstrong, swung harder than Morton's, and it did so in a new way. Oliver was a warmly inventive cornet player, whose vividly conceived solo on "Dippermouth Blues," notable for its swing and coherence, was memorized by scores of trumpet players. Known for his sweet, dark tone, for his expressive blues, and for his facility with mutes, he was an effective accompanist to blues singers as late as 1928. Most importantly, he was a bandleader with a firm conception of his music. His band was "well drilled," according to an early admirer, the New Orleans guitarist Dr. Edmond

Souchon (1897–1968). And he was the musical and personal idol of the remarkable Louis Armstrong.

Souchon first heard Oliver in 1907, he remembered, when, as a young
white boy, he snuck down to Storyville to a club called the "Big 25," where
Oliver was performing a music Souchon later said was "rough, rugged, and
contained many bad chords." The youngster also heard in the Oliver band a
"drive" and rhythm, a "wonderfully joyous New Orleans sound . . . in all its
beauty" (Souchon, "King Oliver: A Very Personal Memoir," in *Jazz Panorama*). As
Oliver was born in or around New Orleans in 1885, he would have been twenty-
two when Souchon heard him. Oliver was then playing in cabarets, but also in
brass bands and dance bands. He stayed in New Orleans, working at times as a
butler, until 1918, when he left for Chicago. Two years later, he was leading his
own band, which he took on the road as far as San Francisco in 1921. In June
1922, King Oliver's Creole Jazz Band opened at the Lincoln Gardens in Chicago.
The band was not ethnically "Creole." King Oliver was not Creole, nor were the
Dodds brothers, clarinetist Johnny and drummer Warren "Baby" Dodds, and
certainly Louis Armstrong was not—the group was dubbed Creole because of
the supposedly greater prestige of light-skinned Creoles. It was this band,
joined by Louis Armstrong in July, that was to make musical history. Besides

Publicity pose of King Oliver's Creole Jazz Band, 1923. From left: Honore Dutrey,
Baby Dodds (note old style drum set), Oliver (standing, with plunger mute), Louis
Armstrong (kneeling, with slide trumpet, a novelty which he never used on records),
Lil Hardin, Bill Johnson, Johnny Dodds. (Courtesy Rutgers Institute of Jazz Studies)

Oliver, Armstrong, and the Dodds brothers, it contained Lil Hardin on piano, Honore Dutrey on trombone, and Bill Johnson on banjo and string bass.

Souchon said that the Creole Jazz Band was no longer playing pure New Orleans music. The tempos were sometimes faster and the arrangements more complex than one would expect to have heard in a New Orleans dance hall, or on a bandstand by the shores of Lake Pontchartrain. Oliver's music was highly organized: He included in his arrangements a variety of effects, such as the breaks by two cornets that astounded Chicagoans. (In a break the rhythm section stops and a soloist—or in this case two—plays a two- or four-bar solo.) The recordings sound so spontaneous that many fans assumed that they were wholly improvised. In fact, the Oliver band's routines were carefully rehearsed.

The impact of this band was immediate and profound: A whole generation of young white musicians, for instance, was inspired by the King Oliver band at Lincoln Gardens. The influence spread with recordings. On April 5 and 6, 1923 (according to the latest research), the band gathered in Richmond, Indiana, where they recorded for the first time, making nine sides in two days for the Gennett label. The first, "Just Gone," is a bouncy Oliver original distinguished by the occasional singing lines of Johnny Dodds and the jaunty rhythmic variety of the cornets in the last choruses.

The second piece recorded, "Canal Street Blues," is a marvel. After a brightly played four-bar introduction, it stomps off spaciously, the trumpets in graceful interplay with Dodd's clarinet and with each other. Armstrong and Oliver trade high-spirited little riffs back and forth. Later Johnny Dodds solos brilliantly for two 12-bar choruses over Bill Johnson's banjo, Lil Hardin's Morton-ish piano, and Baby Dodds's woodblocks. The final choruses are given over to the ensemble. At this point in jazz history, this was the hardest swinging piece ever recorded.

The session did not end there. After two less impressive tunes, one ("I'm Going Away to Wear You Off My Mind") featuring a solo chorus by Lil Hardin, the band made "Chimes Blues," which included a solo by Armstrong, a carefully organized little bit that is striking despite its brevity. (See music example.)

Armstrong has a written theme to play here, in two 12-bar choruses. Within those constraints, he is distinctive for his warm sound, clear attack and relaxed swing. He improvises a little in measures 9 and 10 of each chorus, as shown. The piece got its name from the piano chimes effects that precede Armstrong's solo. "Weather Bird Rag" began the next session on April 6: It is notable for the variety of its breaks, including two by the harmonized horns of Oliver and Armstrong. At the Lincoln Gardens, Oliver and Armstrong would play breaks like these nightly. Always coordinated and always different, they amazed and puzzled the crowd. Later Armstrong revealed the secret: Oliver would either hum the next break to Armstrong in the middle of the chorus, or finger, without blowing, the phrase he wanted the younger man to pick up. Remarkably, Armstrong was able to produce a harmony for what Oliver had intimated on the spot. The two cornets are clearly audible on "Snake Rag" from the same session, as is Honore Dutrey's slide trombone. In the tailgate style he

Example 4–3.
Louis Armstrong's solo on "Chimes Blues."

was using, the trombone slides up to the note it wants: The glissandos that result are both melodic and rhythmic devices. "Frog-i-More" (also known as "Froggie Moore"), written by Jelly Roll Morton in 1918, is notable for Armstrong's prominent cornet.

The Oliver band's most famous piece, "Dippermouth Blues" (credited to both cornetists), was recorded first on the same session of April 6, 1923, and then again on June 23, 1923. A comparison of the two versions reveals much about the nature of improvisation in early jazz. In general, the most fruitful method of studying improvisation is to compare takes made the same day or, as in this case, versions made at different times, noting the similarities and differences in the solos. On the first version, which is included in the revised SCCJ (the first edition had the June recording), "Dippermouth" moves brightly from the beginning, with the two cornets sounding relaxed as they introduce the melody while Dodds, clearly at home in this piece, plays beautifully decorative figures around them. After Dodds's solo, Armstrong takes over the lead, and his vigorous phrases lead to Oliver's solo. (See music example.)

Typical of Oliver's style in its forthright rhythms, and in its clever manipulation of sounds, this solo remains striking for its coherence, for the way each phrase seems to demand its successor which, when Oliver plays it, seems inevitable. Its three choruses make a single, joyous statement. In the swing era, when bands played "Dippermouth"—by then it was known under Fletcher Henderson's title "Sugarfoot Stomp"—they typically assigned Oliver's solo to a single trumpet, or rearranged it for trumpet choir. It became an integral part of the piece.

The second "Dippermouth Blues" is faster and was recorded with greater clarity. Again Oliver and Dodds take solos, producing statements very close to their choruses in April. The beginning bars of each of Oliver's three choruses remain about the same, suggesting that the building of intensity we hear at

Example 4–4.
King Oliver's solo on "Dippermouth Blues" (April 1923). (Double bar indicates new chorus.) Note the key; many reissues play flat.

those moments in each chorus was the most "prepared" part of the solo. In the early version, Dodds played two different choruses, building from the first into the second. At the June recording, Dodds plays a first chorus similar to that of the earlier version – and then repeats that statement verbatim! Today, one might think it more natural to expect that the later clarinet solo would be more varied, not less, since Dodds was more familiar with the piece by then. But in the twenties, a different esthetic prevailed. Especially for recordings, musicians tried to perfect their statements beforehand, and if they found something they liked, they repeated it. Even outside the studio, the evidence suggests that the repetition of one's best ideas was not frowned upon as it would be later in jazz history.

The blues appears to have been the forum for the most relaxed and extended improvisation, judging from early jazz recordings. This drives home how important the blues was to the formation of jazz, not only as repertory but as a language, that is, as a source of melodic ideas, and as a vehicle for improvisation. "Dippermouth" is only one of many recordings in 12-bar blues form that break away from the ensemble emphasis of early jazz to present a few soloists. "Camp Meeting Blues" is another one in the Oliver discography of 1923. Two takes of "Every Saturday Night," recorded by Bernie Young's Creole Jazz Band in October 1923 in Chicago (notice the use of *Creole* again in the band's name), consist primarily of strings of solos. And "Play That Thing," discussed below, does as well. It would be difficult to find non-blues recordings in 1923 that featured so many solos.

The recording technology was primitive. Until 1925, recording was "acoustical"—musicians played into a large horn like the one in the old Victor Records advertisement showing a dog listening to a record. Recordings were cut directly onto discs—if mistakes were made, the band would have to start on a new disc. To achieve something like balance, the engineers would actually move musicians around the room, or urge them to play more loudly or softly. Louis Armstrong said that because of his big sound he had to stand well behind Oliver in these recordings so as not to overpower his mentor. The major innovations in recording technology were the invention of microphones ("electrical recording") in 1925, creating a marked improvement in sound quality, and, a little before 1950, tape recordings and the long playing record, both of which allowed one for the first time to record uninterrupted music lasting longer than four minutes.

The Oliver band recorded blues, rags, stomps, and an occasional popular tune. The march "High Society," one of their best known recordings, is discussed in Chapter 5. In early October, 1923, the band recorded with New Orleans clarinetist Jimmie Noone replacing Johnny Dodds. A smoother technician, Noone rarely played with the force of Dodds: He made up for it with the fluidity of his lines. Noone can be heard to advantage on "Chattanooga Stomp" and "Camp Meeting Blues."

He can be heard as well on a 1923 recording featuring another New Orleans cornetist, Tommy Ladnier (1900–1939). On "Play That Thing," Noone proves to be a suave blues player, while Ladnier, a cornetist in some ways comparable to Oliver, takes a solo in the mid-range of the trumpet, and proves that Oliver was not the only master of wa-wa mutes. (A bit of Ladnier's soloing with Ma Rainey is transcribed in Appendix 1.) Later, Noone, who was with Dodds and Sidney Bechet one of the most important clarinetists of the period, would take classical clarinet lessons—from the same teacher as Benny Goodman—and would perform in 1928 in a newly elegant style with a band that featured the piano sensation Earl Hines.

As Lawrence Gushee has pointed out, the King Oliver band did not exactly break up. Its personnel kept changing until in 1924, it was a new organization with a different sound. Bill Johnson was the first to leave. By the end of 1923 the Dodds brothers and Honore Dutrey were gone. Prodded by Lil Hardin, Louis Armstrong went out on his own in June 1924, and Hardin, now married to Armstrong, followed in September. Oliver continued with a group he called his Dixie Syncopators, and they made several satisfying records, including "Snag It" of March 1926, and "Someday, Sweetheart," of the following September. (This last has a lovely tuba line by Bert Cobb, clearly audible because of the new electrical recording technology.) Oliver's technique deteriorated steadily after that, probably because of gum troubles, and by 1928 he sometimes let other trumpeters play lead on his records. But that same year he accompanied singer Hazel Smith in two numbers which are buoyed by his sensitive phrases. His crying blues lines, modest by Armstrong's standards, have a kind of dark dignity that succeeding trumpeters rarely equalled.

Oliver continued to play and tour into the thirties. But by 1936, he was broke in Savannah, Georgia, working in ill health in a pool hall, yet determined to return to music. He died there on April 8, 1938, but was buried in Woodlawn Cemetery, Bronx, New York. To some his death must have seemed anticlimactic. The jazz world had largely passed him by a decade before. By 1923, when he made his last records with his Creole Jazz Band, the future already belonged to a younger generation, led by the likes of Sidney Bechet and, preeminently, by Louis Armstrong.

5 Sidney Bechet

Born in New Orleans in 1897, clarinetist and soprano saxophonist Sidney Bechet was in 1923 arguably the most daring soloist in jazz until, soon afterwards, he was matched by his lifelong rival, Louis Armstrong. In the early twenties, Bechet was playing with a then unparalleled rhythmic drive and technical skill. He was improvising more freely than most other jazz musicians. In 1923, as we have seen in Oliver's recordings, jazz players tended to think of a solo as a set piece, an original composition to be worked on and polished up in private and to be played in roughly the same way at each performance. Although the difference may best be seen as a change in emphasis rather than a complete break with the past, Bechet and Armstrong improvised their solos more fully, and influenced others to follow in what turned out to be the way of the future.

Bechet was discovered when he was around six. (That is, according to Bechet's extraordinary autobiography, *Treat It Gentle*, which is the source of all of his statements in this chapter.) He started as a clarinetist by surreptitiously picking up an older brother's clarinet: According to legend and to his own testimony, his first tune was the prophetic "I Don't Know Where I'm Going, But I'm On My Way." He had gained some measure of competence when his mother planned a birthday party for his older brother Leonard, an amateur trombone player who was studying to be a dentist. Mrs. Bechet hired Freddie Keppard's band to provide the music. The clarinetist didn't show up, but people started to hear, softly in the background, a clarinet sweetly improvising. They looked into the office area, and there in the dentist's chair, was the young Bechet.

He was rarely willing to take a back seat again. In the New Orleans ensembles that nurtured Bechet and Armstrong, the cornetist was more or less constrained to paraphrasing the melody, often selecting at the same time appropriate ornamental notes. The trombonist created a slower countermelody based on chord progressions, while the clarinetist, the least concerned with the written melody, played florid <u>obbligatos (decorative passages)</u>, using scales and arpeggios. Bechet was unwilling to stay in this role. He developed the clarinet part further until—at least in his hands—it rivalled or actually dominated the cornetist.

Many New Orleans clarinetists played with a rich, packed, woody sound. Bechet would have this sound during his whole career. Sometimes this sound was achieved at the sacrifice of some fluency, but New Orleans clarinetists also valued speed and grace. The most famous clarinet solo in their tradition is actually a transcribed piccolo solo from "High Society," adapted from a published Robert Recker arrangement by Alphonse Picou and then memorized by generations of New Orleans clarinetists who, depending on their skill and predilections, would play it as written or adapt it to their needs. "High Society" was first recorded in 1923 by the King Oliver band with Johnny Dodds on clarinet. The solo is in a 32-bar ABAC form, and Dodds plays the first half of the solo (AB) as shown in the example. (See music example.)

Example 5–1.
"High Society" clarinet solo, first 15 measures as played by Johnny Dodds.

What one hears in Sidney Bechet's early work is a virtuoso extension of this New Orleans clarinet tradition. As a boy, Bechet was immersed in that tradition. He had lessons from Creole clarinetists Lorenzo Tio, Big Eye Louis Nelson, and George Baquet. He marched in parades with the bands, and played with John Robichaux's genteel dance orchestra. He did this work mainly from his ear. Bechet never became a good reader, and in his maturity was sensitive about this failing. But he seemed able to pick up any tune immediately.

The precocious youth's apprenticeship in New Orleans was thorough. After working in New Orleans with Bunk Johnson and King Oliver, Bechet led from 1914 to 1917 an itinerant life, touring in shows and going as far north as Chicago, where he frequently teamed with Freddie Keppard, a clannish, difficult man, a hard-drinker with whom the usually prickly Bechet got on perfectly.

In Chicago, according to his biographer John Chilton (*Sidney Bechet: The Wizard of Jazz*), Bechet performed in a duo with Tony Jackson, a pianist who was lavishly praised by Jelly Roll Morton. In this duo at least, Bechet must have been playing lead.

In 1919, black composer and violinist Will Marion Cook brought his New York Syncopated Orchestra, a large band with a large choir, to Chicago, heard Bechet, and managed to hire him as a soloist. Bechet toured with Cook, arriving finally in New York early in 1919. Cook's was a versatile group with a wide-ranging repertoire. Cook would feature Bechet playing the blues in programs that included everything from "Joshua Fit the Battle of Jericho" to transcriptions of Brahms's Hungarian Dances. In June 1919, Bechet joined Cook for a tour of Europe, where he received a prescient review by the Swiss conductor Ernest Ansermet, who, after hearing Bechet play his feature—"Characteristic Blues"—wrote:

> There is in the Southern Syncopated Orchestra an extraordinary clarinet virtuoso who is, so it seems, the first of his race to have composed perfectly formed blues on the clarinet. I've heard two of them which he had elaborated at great length . . . They are equally admirable for their richness of invention, force of accent, and daring in novelty and the unexpected. Already, they gave the idea of a style, and their form was gripping, abrupt, harsh, with a brusque and pitiless ending like that of Bach's second Brandenburg Concerto. I wish to set down the name of this artist of genius: as for myself, I shall never forget it—it is Sidney Bechet.

Ansermet concluded that Bechet's style "is perhaps the highway the whole world will swing along tomorrow." (Originally in *Revue Romande,* October 1919. Translated by Walter Schaap in 1938.) Bechet recorded a "Characteristic Blues" with Noble Sissle in 1937 that is probably the same piece that Ansermet heard.

While in London with Cook's orchestra, Bechet picked up a straight soprano saxophone and soon developed on this difficult instrument one of the most extravagant—and least polite—sounds in jazz: a broad, wailing cry, openly and sometimes throbbingly emotional. Bechet's clarinet playing was warm, woody, and intimate, despite the broad vibrato. His tone on soprano was larger, smoother, and more romantic. He mused on clarinet; on soprano he soared recklessly. Soon he was overwhelming almost any ensemble he played with. He would start a chorus by hitting a high, throbbing note with a vibrato so broad and fast it sounded like a trill, descend with a whinnying stutter, grumble in the lower register, twirl around with little triplet figures and rip back upwards again, traversing over an octave in a single, dramatic rush. To emphasize a high note, he might add a grace note an octave below.

He liked to talk about music as if it had a will of its own: The job of the musician was to find out where the music wanted to go. But in his own playing he drove the music before him, especially in his last choruses. The marvelous "Maple Leaf Rag" of 1932 ends with several choruses of roof-raising fervor that seemed to surprise all the players except Bechet himself. He knew how to build a performance chorus by chorus, so that he always made a splash at the end. He loved melodies, including some that seem corny today. By the fifties, "La Vie en Rose," "Dear Old Southland," and even "Swanee River" were a regular part of his repertoire.

Bechet returned to New York from Europe late in 1922. On July 30, 1923, he went into the studio to make his first surviving recordings. (An earlier session with Bessie Smith was lost.) These were led by Clarence Williams, a pianist and songwriter who was also active as a music publisher and record producer. (Williams was almost certainly born in 1898, although some sources say 1893. He died in 1965.) "Kansas City Man Blues" is a 12-bar blues whose theme is stated by Bechet in vibrant long tones and sharp yips. The more reticent cornetist, Thomas Morris, is overwhelmed by Bechet's wonderfully vocalistic approach to the blues—vocalistic especially in its rhythmic freedom. In measure four of the first and second choruses, Bechet plays a characteristic descending formula, which will reappear in later solos. (See music example.)

Example 5–2.
Sidney Bechet's formula from "Kansas City Man Blues."

Bechet often ends a chorus, as he does on "New Orleans Hop Scop Blues" from October 1923, with a major third, which helps to resolve the tension created by the preceding "blue" thirds. This strategy returns on later records: It appears twice during the first chorus of his 1944 recording, "Blue Horizon" (SCCJ). "New Orleans Hop Scop Blues," a 12-bar form, has a boogie-woogie feeling from the third chorus on. In the final chorus Bechet develops several distinctive ideas he introduced in the fourth, illustrating his unusually strong awareness of the overall form of a piece. (See music example.)

Example 5–3.
Sidney Bechet's motive from "New Orleans Hop Scop Blues."

About a year later, in October 1924, Bechet joined Louis Armstrong on a Clarence Williams date that produced "Texas Moaner Blues." Listening to that recording, one is immediately struck by the unusual equality of the three lead voices: Armstrong, Bechet (on clarinet) and Charles Irvis on trombone. Armstrong's solo is notable for its rhythmic variety and because it has some of the freedom from the beat that characterizes Bechet's early work. Bechet switches to

Clarence Williams (at piano) and orchestra, about 1927, with saxophonist Prince Robinson (standing), singer Eva Taylor, and trombonist Charlie Irvis. (Courtesy Rutgers Institute of Jazz Studies)

the louder soprano sax for his urgent solo, with its powerful vibrato, throat growls and wailing blue notes.

Bechet recorded with Armstrong again on December 17, 1924, and then made some of the most glorious minutes in all of jazz on January 8, 1925. The unlikely vehicle was the Clarence Williams publication "Cake Walkin' Babies From Home." (SCCJ) A cakewalk was a strutting circle dance in which black couples marched about in what seems to have been originally a parody of upper-class whites. It was celebrated in Will Cook's musical, *Clorindy, or the Origin of the Cakewalk* (1898), and must have seemed quaintly nostalgic by the twenties. "Cake Walkin' Babies" celebrates those "struttin' syncopators." The sprightly voice of Eva Taylor lights up this pop song, but the joy of the performance comes with the last two ensemble choruses, during which the intensely competitive Bechet and Armstrong push and prod each other in a kind of incandescent free-for-all.

It's a masterpiece of what we might call the new New Orleans style. After a couple of stunning Bechet breaks, Armstrong suddenly explodes with several repeated notes, higher and louder than anything he had played before. They sound like a wake-up call to the jazz age. He seemed to be inventing a new, harder kind of swing by an act of will. Later, Bechet would talk from his unique perspective about what made these sessions so valuable: "We were working together. Each person, he was the other person's music: you could feel that really running through the band, making itself up and coming out so new and strong" (*Treat It Gentle*, p. 176).

The period of Bechet's greatest fame in this country came after he started recording under his own name for Victor and for Blue Note in the thirties. There were periods of discouragement and inactivity as well in this decade. For a while, he and his friend, trumpeter Tommy Ladnier, ran a tailor shop in New York. In 1932, Bechet and Ladnier met in more promising circumstances, to record six numbers for Victor, including the "Maple Leaf Rag" already mentioned. After a six-year gap, during which he worked primarily with the Noble Sissle dance band, Bechet recorded again with Ladnier. Their "Really the Blues," written by the second clarinetist on the date, Milton "Mezz" Mezzrow, become something of a hit. During 1939 and 1940, Bechet recorded regularly with a quartet that included the young Kenny Clarke, soon to be a formative drummer of modern jazz. These titles include some rare Bechet vocals. The relaxed and informal "Sidney's Blues" has him singing with amateur verve about a cat who stood up "and talked like a natural man."

He was adventurous in other ways. In 1939, he recorded with New York stride pianist Willie "the Lion" Smith and drummer Zutty Singleton a group of rhumbas and Haitian meringues, with their infectious Carribean dance rhythms. Uncharacteristically, Bechet subsumes himself to the music, simply playing the melodies and appropriate harmony parts. Although he would never record this repertoire again, he probably heard predecessors of such material while growing up in New Orleans.

He also recorded in 1939 his celebrated "Summertime" for Blue Note. "Summertime" was a somewhat controversial choice for a recording by Bechet: Even in 1939, some diehard New Orleans jazz fans believed their heroes should stick to classics of the New Orleans tradition rather than venture into playing popular songs. Bechet's playing should have silenced any criticism. He performs on soprano, beginning with a sweetly restrained statement of the melody. Bechet holds his vibrato in check until the second chorus, when he suddenly growls menacingly down low, and then opens up, rising in pitch, volume and intensity until the striking break with which the piece ends. Just as potent is the 1944 blues "Blue Horizon," mentioned above (SCCJ). On "Blue Horizon," Bechet plays—one is tempted to say sings—with slow-motion dignity, bending notes, moving pensively through the low *chalumeau* register of the clarinet and building up to long high notes of hair-raising intensity. Behind Bechet, one can hear the bowed bass, a New Orleans tradition.

In 1941, Bechet created two curiosities for Victor—Mezz Mezzrow calls them outrages—recording "Sheik of Araby" and "Blues of Bechet" as a one-man band. In a pioneering use of overdubbing, he plays as many as six instruments himself. Perhaps he discovered that he was not his own ideal accompanist. Although he later complained that the sides would have been better if he had rehearsed more fully with the recording engineer, he never repeated the experiment.

Some Blue Note sessions later in the forties were marred by a trite Dixieland background and by stiff drumming. But the 1945 date with New Orleans old-timer Bunk Johnson was memorable. Born in 1879, Johnson had become important in the Dixieland revival, which we discuss in Chapter 12. With Bechet, he plays an unassuming lead on the bouncy "Lord, Let Me in the Lifeboat," and on the blues, "Days Beyond Recall."

Sidney Bechet in a publicity shot for his one-man band records, 1941. (Courtesy Rutgers Institute of Jazz Studies)

Bechet preferred Johnson's modest approach to playing the melody to Armstrong's power and agile control. Unhappy about a reunion record date with Armstrong made for Decca in 1940, he wrote: "It seemed like he was wanting to make it a kind of thing where we were supposed to be bucking each other, competing instead of working together for that real feeling that would let the music come new and strong." When on January 17, 1945, Bechet returned to New Orleans, for the first time since 1919, he joined Armstrong for an all-star concert in the Municipal Auditorium. Their segment together, heard on a radio broadcast, was marred by the competition between the two stars. Armstrong complained at rehearsal that Bechet was trying to play lead.

In what would be his last attempt to form a New Orleans-style band with his peers, Bechet formed a working band in 1945 with Bunk Johnson. The attempt foundered when Johnson seemed to prefer drinking to playing, at least to playing with the difficult Bechet. Perhaps it was doomed from the beginning: The band could not find bookings in New York. During March and April, they played in Boston's Savoy Cafe. They received some publicity. Before Johnson left, the band made regular broadcasts in Boston, including a few interviews. The issued broadcasts find Johnson sounding sometimes ill-at-ease, or simply

Sidney Bechet (left) and Bunk Johnson (right) in Boston, 1945. Pops Foster is the bassist. (Courtesy Rutgers Institute of Jazz Studies)

overwhelmed: He is easily outplayed by the younger and more virtuosic Bechet, who does little to accomodate the trumpeter's gentler style. After weeks of bickering over Bechet's overbearing soprano saxophone, which Johnson disdained in favor of the clarinet, the trumpeter was replaced by the teenaged Johnny Windhurst. In the meantime, some of the best surviving music from this period was broadcast on April 10, 1945, when Bechet played long solos without a trumpeter present.

During the war, Bechet had played in New Orleans revivalist and Dixieland clubs around New York such as Jimmy Ryan's and Nick's. Despite the changing styles of jazz—bebop had arrived in 1944—he worked steadily in this country. John Chilton has written in his definitive biography that not a week of 1946 went by in which Bechet didn't play a concert. (Chilton, *Sidney Bechet*) He played brilliantly. His power and virtuosity in the forties can be heard by listening to his various recordings of "China Boy." In 1940 with cornetist Muggsy Spanier, he drives his solo for chorus upon chorus, without a drummer. At a 1946 Town Hall concert with New Orleans bassist Pops Foster and drummer Baby Dodds, and James P. Johnson at the piano, he plays "China Boy" at a slightly slower pace—the only passage similar to the earlier version comes at the start of the last chorus in each case. This was obviously a routine of Bechet's, but a dazzling one. The last chorus of the 1946 performance, transcribed in the example, begins with this routine and continues with some rhythmic trickery that sounds surprisingly modern. (See music example.)

Bechet began teaching in 1947. One of his students was soprano saxophonist Bob Wilber, now a leading force in traditional jazz. Bechet was working steadily, but didn't enjoy the stardom of Louis Armstrong: not until he made his

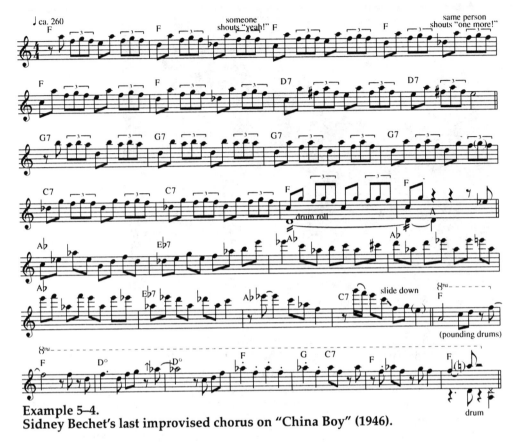

Example 5–4.
Sidney Bechet's last improvised chorus on "China Boy" (1946).

permanent home in France where, after successful tours in 1949 and 1950, he emigrated in 1951.

He was adored there: The Rue Bechet was named after him, and his wedding in 1951 was covered by the press as if he were royalty. He recorded prolifically in the fifties, mostly for the Vogue label, usually with a young band of Frenchman Claude Luter, who turned the musical direction over to Bechet while treating the older man as, according to Bob Wilber, a kind of capricious god. In his earlier career, Bechet did not compose much, but in France he had a hit with his throbbing ballad "Petite Fleur," which he recorded in 1952. The tune's sentimental performance appealed to the French. No wonder: In this mood, with his wide vibrato and broadly emotional approach to melody, Bechet was the Edith Piaf of the soprano saxophone. "Petite Fleur" and another Bechet tune, "Les Oignons," became pop-jazz standards in France.

Bechet was also interested in another kind of composition. To a story line by Andre Coffrant, he wrote a ballet, "La Nuit Est Une Sorcière," which he performed in 1953. It's really a collaboration, as Bechet produced the themes, which were orchestrated by James Toliver. The results were mixed, with at times amateurish string writing giving way to appealing themes that stand out embarrassedly, as if surprised to be found in such high-toned company. The 1955 production of this ballet was a failure. A second "rapsodie-ballet," this one named "La Colline du Delta," fared no better: It was not recorded until 1964, five years after Bechet's death.

Disappointed by the fate of these larger works, Bechet nonetheless performed regularly in the early fifties. His work at times settled into a routine. The saxophonist would sometimes devote whole evenings to popular songs and dixieland chestnuts, and his solos were often set pieces. He was still thrilling when placed in challenging settings. At the 1958 Brussels World Fair, paired with swing trumpeter Buck Clayton, he played "Indiana" and "St. Louis Blues" with the relentless vigor that Ernest Ansermet had heard in Bechet 40 years earlier. (That concert was recorded by Columbia Records.)

He was living boldly: He kept separate establishments for his wife and mistress. In 1956, Bechet discovered he was ill with lung cancer. He kept performing until December 20, 1958, where at the Salle Wagram he ended his last set with "Maryland, My Maryland," and then defiantly went out to spend the rest of the night in cabarets. He died on May 14, 1959, the day of his sixty-second birthday.

Bechet was enigmatic, a proud, and by most accounts, often fierce man, habitually courtly but occasionally dangerous. He was jailed in 1929 and subsequently deported from France over a shooting incident. Typically for the romantic Bechet, a woman was at the heart of the argument. The usually generous bassist Pops Foster in his autobiography called Bechet "the most selfish, hard to get along with guy I ever worked with" (p. 169). But Bob Wilber remembers his patient, though demanding lessons, and is still grateful to Bechet for recording with his band of teenagers in 1947. In *Treat It Gentle*, which he dictated in his last years and which was published posthumously, he admitted: "Oh, I can be mean—I know that. But not to the music. That's a thing you gotta trust. You gotta mean it, and you gotta treat it gentle." (p. 5). One of the great tensions in his life was between his natural competitiveness and his lifelong desire to assemble a collectively swinging New Orleans band. He never quite succeeded. Indeed his commanding style as well as his personality made such a success impossible. But he never gave up.

His autobiography tells why. Jazz, or ragtime as he persisted in calling it, had its own needs, its own way, which was intimately related to the history and future of African-American people. Playing it took the utmost sensitivity to other musicians and to the music itself, for the music will tell you which way to go in your life, and what you can feel: "When you're really playing *ragtime*, you're feeling it out, you're playing to the other parts, you're waiting to understand what the other man's doing, and then you're going with his feeling, adding what you have of your feeling. You're not trying to steal anything and you're not trying to fight anything." Bechet disliked big band music, which denied this process of feeling things out by forcing men to read parts rather than improvise. He explained, "All that closeness of speaking to another instrument, to another man—it's gone" (*Treat It Gentle*, p. 211).

For all his seeming conservatism, Bechet insisted that the music must develop. He scorned the Dixielanders who wanted to fix the music's style and repertoire. After all, he had recorded on the sarrusophone, which is like a metal bassoon, in 1924 ("Mandy, Make Up Your Mind," with Clarence Williams and Armstrong), and he made the overdubbing experiments discussed above. "You just can't keep the music unless you move with it," he said. Perhaps in the interest of moving with the music, Bechet recorded in 1957 with the French modernist, Algerian-born pianist Martial Solal. He played sophisticated show tunes with the same bursting-at-the-seams exuberance with which he menaced Armstrong in the twenties. He wrote that the goal of his music was "to reach straight out to life." He might have written his own epitaph when he said that Duke Ellington was "a man with a life in him" (*Treat It Gentle,* p. 143).

6 Louis Armstrong

It would be difficult to overestimate the importance of Louis Armstrong. The music's first genius, as he's been called, Armstrong emerged from King Oliver's band in 1924 and soon became the dominant force in jazz. In dramatic, well shaped solos that have the emotional power of gutbucket blues and the elegance of baroque dances, he taught the music world what swing was and what jazz could become. His solos seem direct, inevitable, clear, and yet they continually surprise. The prestige of his Hot Five and Hot Seven recordings of the mid-twenties made it inevitable that jazz would become a soloist's art. He extended the range and technique of the trumpet, his tone and vibrato still seem miraculous, and he was one of jazz's definitive singers.

Musicians recognized his importance immediately. The biographers of cornetist Bix Beiderbecke, Evans and Sudhalter, wrote about Armstrong's impact: "But it was only with the emergence of Louis Armstrong that the idea of the virtuoso jazz trumpet or cornet solo found definitive expression. With Armstrong, the instrument freed itself entirely from the restrictions of its original marching and circus-band role. When Bix heard Louis later in Chicago, [cornetist Esten] Spurrier said, he realized that King Oliver's young protégé had 'departed greatly from all cornet players . . . in his ability to compose a close-knit, individual 32 measures with all phrases compatible with each other—all the while based on the fundamental tune and chord structure being played. It evoked amazement and envy in all of us' " (*Bix: Man and Legend*, p. 51).

Others admired Armstrong's incomparable tone, with its broad vibrato, a tone that he could still produce—and which was still effective—in his sixties. Armstrong sometimes sang as he played, in horn-like solos that had a vigorous good-humor that was consistently musical. He could sing ballads as well as novelty numbers: His warmth and sincerity on "Sweet Lorraine" (1957) is as impressive as his comicality on "You Rascal You" (1931 and others). He became one of America's great entertainers, known as much, it is said, for his singing as for his trumpet, loved for his jokes and endearing stage mannerisms as well as for his playing. Those mannerisms have made people—black and white—uneasy. Some have criticized Armstrong's place in the entertainment world, as if jazz were ever in this country unconnected to that world. Armstrong's biographer, James Lincoln Collier, in a sometimes condescending book, opines that the audiences that adored Armstrong loved him only for his singing and for his jokes, and describes him as an insecure man who became the helpless victim of a crass entertainment world. He was helpless, it is suggested, because he was always searching for the father he never had. A man of great and varied talents, and of great integrity, Armstrong, we feel certain, would have found such opinions incomprehensible. He did not separate his music making from his entertaining, or his trumpet playing from his singing. Collier criticized Armstrong for his supposedly compulsive work habits, his obsessive need for applause. When Armstrong talked about his career, he merely pointed to his horn and said, "That's my living, and that's my life."

Many of his career choices were made to protect that life in music. These include his decison to work with manager Joe Glaser, who took control of Armstrong's career in the thirties and managed him until the end of Glaser's life, a few years before Armstrong's own demise. Collier suggests that Armstrong was attracted to Glaser because the manager was a tough, loud-talking man, the next thing to a gangster: a surrogate father. But Armstrong remembered being advised when still a boy in New Orleans to get a white man to run his business. Then he would be able to concentrate on his horn. Although that advice might pain us today, when African-Americans have made more progress in taking control of their own affairs, it made sense in the 1920's, and Armstrong's willingness to follow it may have made his career possible.

It is fruitless to condescend to Armstrong's audiences as well. His audiences responded to his personality and stage presence because that personality and presence were essential to his music as well. No one came to an Armstrong concert to hear his jokes, but fans laughed at them because they were told with the same exuberant warmth with which Armstrong played and sang. We might regret the showboating solos Armstrong sometimes settled for in the thirties, and criticize his repertoire towards the end of his life. We would prefer that his biggest hit be "Potato Head Blues" from 1927 rather than "Hello Dolly" from 1963. But those who listen to Armstrong sing "Hello Dolly," "Mack the Knife," or even "Blueberry Hill," will hear incomparably personalized versions of popular songs no worse than many of the ones he sang in the thirties. Armstrong was always part of the entertainment world. He became an internationally recognized star without losing his countryish charm. He played for kings, but never forgot his homefolk. Collier criticizes Armstrong for preferring to socialize with blacks, "and not just blacks, but working-class blacks" (*Louis Armstrong,* p. 75). That preference seems to us inevitable. Those who wish that he had been consistently dignified in manner and repertoire are applying standards of seriousness to Armstrong that may never have been conceived had Armstrong not played so sublimely.

Armstrong was born in what was called the "Back o' Town" district in New Orleans. He grew up in grinding poverty, and was raised by his mother Mary Ann, known as Mayann, and by his grandmother. He always said his birthdate was July 4, 1900, but recent research for Gary Giddins's book and film, *Satchmo*, unearthed the actual birthdate, August 1, 1901. His wide mouth earned him the nickname Satchelmouth, later shortened to Satchmo. Another good-natured reference to this feature of his appearance came in the title of the King Oliver recording, "Dippermouth Blues." Such double-edged humorous nicknames were common among African-Americans. Consider, for example, "Dizzy," "Fats," and "Cootie"!

Armstrong must have heard music from the start. He lived for a time down the street from the famous "Funky Butt" Hall where the earliest jazzmen performed, and he "second-lined," followed the marching bands in parades. As a child, he said in his 1954 autobiography, "I started to listen carefully to the different instruments, noticing the things they played and how they played them. That is how I learned to distinguish the differences between Buddy Bolden, King Oliver and Bunk Johnson." (*Satchmo: My Life in New Orleans*, p. 27. An autobiography from 1936, *Swing That Music*, had been ghost-written.) In his early teens, Armstrong sang tenor in an informal vocal quartet—a group of boys who sang on streetcorners for change—but he didn't play an instrument until after January 1, 1913, when he was picked up by the police for firing a pistol the night before, and sent to the Coloured Waifs' Home, a relatively benign reform school directed by Captain Joseph Jones.

There Armstrong was allowed to join the band, and was eventually given a

Louis Armstrong posing with a cornet for the film *New Orleans*, probably in 1946. Notice its squat shape compared to a trumpet. (Courtesy Rutgers Institute of Jazz Studies)

cornet. He probably learned to play the usual marching band repertoire, and perhaps was exposed to the typically florid cornet solos popular at the time. He said he enjoyed recordings of opera arias as well. After his release in 1914, Armstrong worked at a variety of menial jobs, and played cornet on the side. He must have been developing considerable technical skill. Later, Sidney Bechet remembered him playing on his cornet the clarinet solo in "High Society," considered difficult enough for a clarinetist (Bechet, *Treat It Gentle*, p. 92). At other times, he played what he called "figurations," or fancy improvisations on the chord changes. "I was just like a clarinet player," Armstrong said on BBC TV, "like the guys run up and down the horn nowadays, boppin' and things. I was doin' all that, fast fingers and everything, so he [Oliver] used to tell me: 'Play some lead on that horn, boy.' " Armstrong never forgot that advice. He eventually managed to combine a clarinet-like facility and freedom with Oliver's taste and concern for making every note count. And somewhere along the line he developed a broad, singing tone more touching and dramatic than Oliver's own.

Armstrong's first break came in 1917 when King Oliver left the Kid Ory band, then the hottest in New Orleans, giving his chair to his protégé. Armstrong seems to have been an instant success: "The first night I played with Kid Ory's band, the boys were so surprised they could hardly play their instruments for listening to me blow up a storm. But I wasn't frightened one bit. I was doing everything just exactly the way I'd heard Joe Oliver do it." He would continue to do some things the way Oliver did: Armstrong's playing behind blues singers in the twenties owed something to Oliver's, although Oliver, like most players of his generation, tended to stay in a narrower range, playing strictly melodic ideas rather than Armstrong's more technical patterns, with their clarinet-like scales and arpeggios. There was some direct imitation as well: Armstrong drew on Oliver's solo on "Jazzin' Babies Blues" (1923) for phrases he used on "Railroad Blues" (1925). Armstrong recorded Oliver's "West End Blues" in 1928 a few weeks after Oliver did.

In November 1918, Armstrong started working the riverboats. Around the same time, he entered into his first, short-lived marriage. By May 1919, he had left New Orleans to join Fate Marable's band sailing on the Streckfus line out of St. Louis. During the next two years, he would work with this black dance orchestra, learning to read music and to play a varied repertoire. By September 1921, he was back in New Orleans, which he would leave again in the summer of 1922, when he got his big break, a telegram asking him to join Oliver's band in Chicago. The originality of the band's second cornet player must have been evident from the first. On recordings, discussed in Chapter 4, the richness of Armstrong's tone stands in sharp contrast to the more modest sound Oliver produced.

ARMSTRONG WITH FLETCHER HENDERSON

In February 1924, Armstrong married the Oliver band's pianist, Lil Hardin, and it was largely at her urging that he decided to strike out on his own. He left Oliver in June and played around Chicago with other bands before coming to

New York. He joined Fletcher Henderson's band for a year starting in September 1924, when Henderson was leading the most prestigious large jazz band in the East. Arranger Don Redman told of Armstrong's arrival: "[Drummer] Kaiser Marshall had a car and brought us downtown to meet Louis. He was big and fat, and wore high top shoes with hooks in them, and long underwear down to his socks. When I got a load of that, I said to myself, who in the hell is this guy? It can't be Louis Armstrong. But when he got on the bandstand, it was a different story."

We can hear just how different on his first recordings with the band, made on October 7, 1924. Armstrong solos on the novelty number, "Go 'Long Mule." Arranged by Redman, the piece opens with a short "wack-a-doo" introduction by the brass. Then the reeds play eight bars in a kind of jaunty Charleston style. The whole band plays the melody stiffly, and that is followed by a bluesy solo by trombonist Charlie Green. Then comes a series of arranged breaks, including some imitation horse whinnies and mule brays. Suddenly Armstrong shoots out of the ensemble for 14 bars that seem to come from a different world. Like many of the solos he took early in his year with Henderson, it is based on a relatively restricted choice of notes—but it swings mightily, and it saves the piece for modern listeners.

The Henderson style, already formed under arranger Don Redman by the time Armstrong joined the band, under his influence soon shifted its emphasis and appeal. This demonstrates an often overlooked fact: that jazz big bands did not develop directly out of small Dixieland groups. Big band jazz was not created by inflating New Orleans ensembles. Rather, jazz was injected as it were into existing dance bands whose size made New Orleans-style improvisation impractical, and which were already playing a different kind of music. Henderson's band was initially influenced more by ragtime, black Broadway and vaudeville than by jazz styles. The same is true of Henderson himself: There's a famous story, told by singer Ethel Waters, that when she hired Henderson to accompany her, she had to make him listen to piano rolls of stride pianist James P. Johnson so that he could play blues. At the time Henderson felt more at home with the "Tin Pan Alley" songs he had plugged. His musicians read published stock arrangements as well as the original material of Don Redman, and later of a host of others. Redman (1900-1964) must be given considerable credit for the more modern sound the band evolved. A pioneer in jazzing up the big band medium, he learned to write passage-work in the style of jazz solos, he left space for jazz solos, and he began opposing the band's sections, reeds against brass, in a way that would become a cliché of the swing era.

But Armstrong's influence was crucial. Again and again in the next year, Armstrong would repeat the effect of "Go 'Long Mule," bursting out of a suddenly enlivened ensemble. As Armstrong's own facility, grace and power were developing, he seemed to liberate the band. On "Sugarfoot Stomp" recorded on May 29, 1925, shortly before he left the band, we hear an Armstrong who is stronger and more assured than ever. He bases his solo on Oliver's "Dippermouth Blues" solos, yet he is clearly his own person. And the band swings in a fashion that is not found on their pre-Armstrong records.

Several of Armstrong's solos with Henderson seem like important milestones. Henderson recorded "Everybody Loves My Baby" (November 1924) in a recording that marks the first appearance of Armstrong's voice on record. On one of the two issued takes he speaks a few lines at the end. He also takes an urgent solo, based primarily on the notes of a minor chord, and the band follows him ably. In December, Armstrong took a 16-bar solo on "Mandy, Make Up Your Mind."

Example 6–1.
Louis Armstrong's solo on "Mandy, Make Up Your Mind."

The solo energizes the song rhythmically, and builds towards the triumphant leap from the fifth note of the scale up to the tonic just before its end, a leap found also at the end of the 1927 "Wild Man Blues," and on many other subsequent solos. One of Armstrong's gifts was his ability to build logically to those high notes. (A rare alternate take of "Mandy" has an almost identical solo by Armstrong.)

He recorded "Alabamy Bound" in February 1925, three months before "Sugarfoot Stomp." The band swings as a unit, and Armstrong takes a bright solo. He is followed by Coleman Hawkins, often called the "father of the tenor saxophone," who was, partly under Armstrong's influence, changing his slap-tonguing style into the more legato phrasing that would mark his maturity. (The sharp articulations created by slapping the tongue against the reed were popular among saxophonists at that time, but jazz players disowned the practice by the end of the twenties.) Hawkins spoke with awe of Armstrong in *Esquire* magazine, August 1944 (quoted in Panassié, *Louis Armstrong*, p. 61): "It happened a long, long time ago. Around 1925, at the Roseland on Broadway. Fletcher Henderson's band was playing and there were thousands of dancers, all yelling and clapping . . . The high spot came when Louis Armstrong began 'Shanghai Shuffle.' I think they made him play ten choruses. After that piece a dancer lifted Armstrong onto his shoulders. Fletcher Henderson kept on beating out the rhythm on his piano and I stood silent, feeling almost bashful, asking myself if I would ever be able to attain a small part of Louis Armstrong's greatness."

In early November 1925, Armstrong, again urged by his wife, left the Henderson band to return to Chicago. Henderson summed up his relationship with Armstrong in these words (*Record Changer*, July-August 1950, p. 15): "The band gained a lot from Louis, and he gained a lot from us. By that I mean he *really* learned to read in my band, and to read in just about every key. Although it's common today, it wasn't usual at that time to write in such keys as E natural, or D natural, so that Louis had to learn, and did learn, much more about his own horn than he knew before he joined us. You might say that we put the finishing touches on his playing . . . That's how we influenced him. But he influenced the band greatly, too, by making the men really swing-conscious with that New Orleans style of his. The same kind of effect that Coleman Hawkins had on the reeds, that right-down-to-earth swing, with punch and bounce. He surely was an asset to my orchestra." We will come back to Henderson in Chapter 9.

BESSIE SMITH AND THE BLUES SINGERS

While with Henderson in New York, Armstrong regularly made small group records, usually as part of bands organized by Clarence Williams or Henderson to support singers. The results were as various as the singers themselves, but the highlights are grand indeed. That these sessions were so frequent—sometimes two a day—shows that Armstrong's talent was already appreciated. That the results were so various suggests that Armstrong—and jazz—were connected to both the worlds of vaudeville and of the blues. He accompanied the majestic blues singers Ma Rainey and Bessie Smith, and also provided a brilliant backup to the ebullient Alberta Hunter (who used the name Josephine Beatty). The repertoire varied from serious blues to silly vaudeville numbers. He can be found playing on such songs as "The World's Jazz Crazy," "Papa-De-Da-Da," and "I'm a Little Blackbird Looking for a Bluebird." And he can be heard supporting the noblest blues. Armstrong seemed at home with all sorts of singers and songs. His accompaniments were sometimes restrained, often sensitive, and occasionally brilliant. Perhaps even too brilliant. During the last breaks of the rather foolishly bawdy "Anybody Here Want to Try My Cabbage" (December 9, 1924), as Max Jones and Chilton note, "He backs the vocal line with a quiet low-register phrase that is almost as fast as anything he ever played" (From *Louis*, one of the best books on Armstrong, p. 226). Armstrong overwhelms singer Maggie Jones, but the trumpeter was just as often appropriately self-contained. "I ain't gonna play no second fiddle," went one lyric, "I'm used to playing lead." But on most of these sessions, Armstrong was willing to play second fiddle.

Armstrong recorded with Gertrude "Ma" Rainey in October 1924, soon after he arrived in New York. Rainey (1886–1939), though perhaps best known through her sometime protégée, Bessie Smith, was a powerful, dark-voiced singer, who was in show business since she was 12. She appeared around the turn of the century in a show in Columbus, Georgia called "A Bunch of Blackberries," and later, after marrying, toured with the Rabbit Foot Minstrels. She became famous through her recordings in the twenties, and when she did, hired a jazz band to back her show: it once included Coleman Hawkins. Rainey was a powerful singer with a limited range, who sang slow, sometimes lugubrious blues that were lightened by her flexible use of blues inflections, her rhythmic drive and by her occasional expressive growls and bends (An example is in Appendix 1). On "See See Rider" she is accompanied by the band improvising collectively, filling in at the ends of lines.

Armstrong's most celebrated recordings with a blues singer were with the so-called "Empress of the Blues," Bessie Smith (1895–1937). When Armstrong played with Bessie Smith—he recorded with her three times—he found a vocalist with a power comparable to his own. Like Ma Rainey, Smith was a veteran by the twenties. She had toured with the Rabbit Foot Minstrel troupe that included Ma Rainey. Perhaps she learned something of her craft from Rainey, but Smith was a more flexible and dramatic performer with a wider repertoire. By 1919 she had her own act. In 1923 she made her first recordings: One of these, "Down Hearted Blues," was reputed to have sold three quarters of a million copies in its first six months. Soon she was travelling the country in her own Pullman car,

Bessie Smith wearing a wig for a 1923 publicity shot. (Courtesy Rutgers Institute of Jazz Studies)

with her own troupe in tow. A large, powerfully built woman who entranced her audiences, Smith was able to move comfortably in a repertoire that included the tragic "Back Water Blues," the wryly cynical " 'Taint Nobody's Business If I Do," and the boisterous "Hot Time in the Old Town Tonight." Some of her best blues were written by Smith herself, but she could sing popular songs as convincingly as she rendered her own heartfelt laments. On her last session, made in 1933 four years before her death in a car accident, Smith sang "Alexander's Ragtime Band" with a group of swing musicians, and she sang the number with a raucous good cheer that few singers have matched.

On two days in January 1925, Smith made five numbers with Armstrong. The most famous was the first, W.C. Handy's "St. Louis Blues." Armstrong's trumpet seems like a second voice. His rich, logical phrases and broad tone seem as passionate as Smith's own lines. On "Reckless Blues," he uses a wah-wah mute to create an oddly effective, mocking commentary as Smith cries, "Momma wants some lovin' right now." It is Smith who mocks contemptuously on "You've Been a Good Ole Wagon, Daddy, But You Done Broke Down." Armstrong plays a warmly relaxed introduction to "Sobbin' Hearted Blues." And, muted, he sounds appropriately disrespectful behind Smith on a second number on the theme of impotence, "Cold in Hand Blues," but then takes a nobly restrained blues chorus. The last sessions with Smith, in May 1925, coupled Armstrong with trombonist Charlie Green from the Fletcher Henderson band. On "Careless Love," which Handy said he adapted from an itinerant singer's lament, Smith's voice, which seems to shift in color and weight from number to number, sounds toughly extroverted, with a bit of a growl. To Smith, "Careless Love" isn't a lament, but a "song of hate," as the lyric states. Here—indeed everywhere in her work—Bessie Smith projects an image of a tough, independent woman, one more likely to complain of her man's sexual incapacity ("Cold in Hand Blues") than of being lonely, or, when abandoned, likely to pick herself up and go on exuberantly—"I'm a young woman" she sings in her own "Young Woman Blues," and "ain't done runnin' 'round."

THE HOT FIVES AND SEVENS

By November 1925, Armstrong was back in Chicago. At first he joined his wife's band, Lil Armstrong's Dreamland Syncopators, but he would also play with large dance bands led by Erskine Tate and Carroll Dickerson. Also in November, he entered the OKeh studios to record for the first time under his own name, beginning the series of records called the Hot Fives or Hot Sevens, depending on the size of the group. The numerous Hot Fives were recorded between 1925 and 1928. The 11 Hot Seven numbers were all created in May 1927. These recordings today seem timeless, crucial.

Until 1928, when he began playing with Pittsburgh-born Earl Hines, a virtuoso pianist, Armstrong chose to record primarily with New Orleans players of his own generation (or in Ory's case, an older generation), rather than with forward-looking Easterners such as Hawkins or James P. Johnson. Perhaps he did not think of himself as forward-looking, preferring a tightly-knit band from his hometown to a group of would-be revolutionaries in music. The repertoire of the Hot Fives and Sevens was conservative as well. It included a mix of originals by himself and by members of the band (Lil's pieces dominated the first session), 12-bar blues, and some vaudeville novelties such as "That's When I'll Come Back to You." For the first Hot Five session, the Armstrongs gathered in OKeh's studios with Johnny Dodds, clarinet; Kid Ory, trombone; and Johnny St. Cyr, banjo. The three numbers produced at this session were a good beginning, but they only hinted at the brighter splendors to come.

Armstrong was playing a repertoire he was comfortable with among musicians he knew well. That those musicians could not equal either his flashy virtuosity or his emotional depths was perhaps inevitable. Kid Ory was the quintessential tailgate trombonist who created unforgettable swooping lines that drove any ensemble. Johnny Dodds is a more complicated case, who has been called everything from the greatest jazz clarinetist to a simple-minded primitive. He was neither. He was a stubborn individualist with a big, woody tone, who could play a slow or medium tempo blues with tremendous conviction. His melodic lines were an asset to any ensemble, but tend to be overpowered by Armstrong on these records. Lil Hardin Armstrong, a solid if rarely an inspired soloist, deserves more credit than she has gotten. She drives the rhythm section, after all, not only on these records but on the King Oliver ones, and she went on to lead her own groups. She was also responsible for promoting Armstrong's career, and for writing some of his early tunes. The Hot Fives may well have been her idea, and she certainly helped with the arrangements.

It's interesting to compare the Hot Fives with two sessions Ory, Dodds, and Lil Hardin played together with the fine, rather sober trumpeter George Mitchell in July 1926. (One group of four tunes was issued as by the New Orleans Wanderers; the other as by the New Orleans Bootblacks.) These recordings not only have remarkable solos—notably Dodds's on "Perdido Street Blues"—they show what glories New Orleans ensemble playing was capable of in well-matched bands. At the end of each piece, the listener is absorbed in the totality of the ensemble, in the intricate meshing of improvised parts. Perhaps such effects were less likely to occur when the dominating Armstrong was in the studio.

On February 28, 1926, Armstrong recorded an unexpected hit: "Heebie Jeebies," which features an inane lyric that only Armstrong could save. Even he loses patience—he often played fast and loose with lyrics—and he suddenly starts to scat, singing nonsense syllables that seem to make more sense than the original song. A myth developed that the song sheet slipped out of Armstrong's hand, forcing him to improvise. White jazzman Mezz Mezzrow spoke of this recording: "All the hi-de-ho, vo-de-o-do, and boop-boop-a-doo howlers that later sprouted up around the country like a bunch of walking ads for Alka-Seltzer were mostly cheap commercial imitations of what Louis did spontaneously, and with perfect musical sense, on that historic record . . . For months after that you would hear cats greeting each other with Louis' riffs when they

Louis Armstrong's Hot Five, 1925. From left to right: Armstrong (with what appears to be a trumpet, although he was still recording on cornet), Johnny St. Cyr, Johnny Dodds, Kid Ory, Lil Hardin Armstrong. (Courtesy Rutgers Institute of Jazz Studies)

met around town. 'I got the Heebies,' one would yell out, and the other would answer 'I got the Jeebies' " (Mezzrow, *Really the Blues*, p. 104). Armstrong's vocal improvisation was spontaneous, but it surely did not result from an accident. Armstrong said he used to scat as a child with friends. The myth of the dropped songsheet, like most jazz myths, credits fate rather than the musician's bubbling creativity.

Armstrong's groups would make even better music in the next few years. On May 7, 1927, he and Lil would record the first Hot Seven sides with trombonist John Thomas, Johnny Dodds, St. Cyr, Pete Briggs on tuba and Baby Dodds on drums, making "Willie the Weeper" and the misleadingly named "Wild Man Blues," neither wild nor a blues but one of Armstrong's most magisterial slow pieces. (Armstrong previously recorded "Wild Man Blues" under Johnny Dodds's leadership.) Armstrong is sounding more confident and expansive, ranging further and further over his horn. His "Wild Man Blues" begins with him playing the theme rather quietly: In a series of exuberant breaks he ascends in volume, pitch and emotion simultaneously.

Two days later Armstrong was back in the studios to make "Chicago Breakdown" with a 10-piece band including Earl Hines that must have sounded more like the groups he was working with in theaters. "Potato Head Blues" (SCCJ) of May 10 was made with Lil Armstrong back on piano and with the Hot

Seven. It sounds like a masterpiece from the opening ensemble, which has Armstrong stating the theme relaxedly under the active counterpoint of Johnny Dodds. This complicated construction isn't a blues at all. It has a theme A for 32 bars, then theme B (the verse) introduced by a trumpet solo. That is followed by a clarinet solo on the chords of A. Then the banjo introduces a trumpet solo on the chords of A played stoptime, followed by an ensemble ending based on the second half of A. (In a stoptime chorus, the band stops keeping time. They will typically play a single chord together at the first beat of a two-bar segment. Then they will be silent as the soloist fills in the rest of the phrase, only to come in with another thumping chord at the beginning of the next two bars and so on until the end of the chorus. The idea is to leave space for the soloist to display his or her talents.) The practice of playing the verse after one chorus instead of at the outset was common in the twenties. Perhaps the idea was to break up the sequence of repeated choruses. Predictably the highlight of "Potato Head Blues" (SCCJ) is Armstrong's solo over stoptime accompaniment. (See music example.)

Example 6–2.
Louis Armstrong's second solo on "Potato Head Blues." Chords in parentheses are not played by the band, but implied in Armstrong's solo.

The beautifully shaped improvisations Armstrong creates here do not rely on the written melody at all. His relaxed rhythmic feel is created by his triplet-like approach to eighth notes, and by his constant use of syncopations. Most soloists would be more confined by the stoptime background: Armstrong begins by placing his melodies between the punctuation offered every two bars by the band, but gradually he breaks away from that pattern until, by the second half of his solo, he is playing right through the stoptime. He uses register dramatically, placing his high notes at the climax of the solo, the last part of which begins with a long, cleanly hit A, then descends, until he moves to a higher, vibrato-laden C, a thrilling effect.

Armstrong had switched from cornet to trumpet by the time of his recordings of 1928, made in Chicago with Earl Hines on piano and an innovative drummer from New Orleans, Zutty Singleton. His playing now had a brighter sound, and his band's sound had shifted as well. In keeping with the trends of the late twenties, the ensemble work here is fully rehearsed, arranged by Don Redman, with solos only in the featured spots.

The most striking addition to the band was pianist Earl Hines. Hines (1903–1983), born in Pittsburgh, became musical director for Armstrong's Stompers at the Sunset Cafe in 1927. Late that year he began working with clarinetist Jimmy Noone at the Apex Club, and in 1928 began recording influential solos in New York. He became the key pianist in jazz at the time, known for what was called his "trumpet style." With unprecedented dash and abandon, he played hornlike melodies in his right hand, often in octaves for added brilliance. More importantly, his playing was rhythmically complex and full of a surprising amount of dissonance. In a constantly inventive way, he would break up phrases between his two hands at a time when most pianists used their left hand merely to accompany the melodies of their right. His work on his own will be discussed later, but he proved to be a stimulating partner to Armstrong, and an accomplished virtuoso with a wealth of vigorous ideas. His technical skill resulted in the sweeping phrases of his solo on "Save It, Pretty Mama" and in the fascinating, alert interchanges between Armstrong and Hines on "No One Else But You."

Their recordings together include the celebrated "West End Blues" of June 1928, a piece written by King Oliver which in Armstrong's version begins with a dashing opening cadenza that stands out even among the generally brilliant playing Armstrong was doing at the period. Armstrong's solo chorus that follows is a dramatic statement whose effect for modern listeners is diminished by a clumsy trombone chorus succeeding it. A routine in which Armstrong's voice trades phrases with the clarinet livens up the next chorus of this piece. Hines takes a characteristically unpredictable solo after that and then Louis returns. He begins this last chorus with a long held note, and then a four note blues run repeated over and over. This run was heard in the introduction, and it seems that Armstrong is picking up where he left off and tying things together.

The unaccompanied introduction has attracted the most interest and elicited the extravagant praise of Gunther Schuller and others. Hines and others have said that Armstrong thought of playing this introduction in the studio. That may be true, but the music he played came from his previous musical experience, as we will show. His opening is shown in the example. (See music example.)

Example 6–3.
Louis Armstrong's introduction to "West End Blues."

He begins with a fanfare, descending and then ascending in triplets, ending on a long high C. This he follows with an intricate bluesy passage. A similar bluesy passage appears (in the key of B♭ as opposed to E♭ here) during a break on a record Louis made accompanying singer Margaret Johnson in October 1924. The song was "Changeable Daddy of Mine" (See Porter, 1981). Near the end Louis takes a double time break. (See music example.)

Example 6–4.
Louis Armstrong's break near the end of "Changeable Daddy of Mine." The original is in 16th notes and in B♭ major. It is given here in 8th notes and in E♭ major for comparison with the previous example.

Many listeners have commented that the 1928 introduction suggests double time, compared to the tempo of the tune that follows. Significantly, the break on "Changeable Daddy" was part of a double time passage for the whole band. Clearly this was music Louis had under his fingers in different keys by 1928, suggesting that he practiced "licks" in this way, just as today's "serious" jazz artists do. His "West End Blues" set a standard, and posed a challenge, for musicians to come.

Later in 1928 Armstrong recorded an extraordinary duet, "Weather Bird" (SCCJ), with Hines, a fascinating uptempo conversation that was freely based on "Weather Bird Rag," which Armstrong had recorded with Oliver in 1923. In another vein entirely was "Tight Like This," a 16-bar minor key song that begins with an introductory verse by Louis and the band, continues with some piano, and then moves to a three chorus solo by Armstrong. Daring and dramatic, this solo builds relentlessly from its subdued beginning to the virtuosic last chorus. As if to demonstrate that he was the master of all emotional levels, in March 1929 Armstrong recorded with a band of predominantly white musicians—including the great Texas-born trombonist Jack Teagarden—"Knockin' a Jug." After Teagarden's solo (discussed in Chapter 7), Armstrong plays a solo which alternates tense little phrases with the most offhandedly casual tags. It's music with an exquisite balance and maturity.

ARMSTRONG THE CELEBRITY

It was also almost the last small band Armstrong recording for a decade and a half. Armstrong had become a star, and would front his own big band until 1944. He recorded regularly, playing arrangements designed frankly to feature his singing and trumpet playing. This trumpet playing took on an added luster, but the results were often less satisfying than the music he made in the twenties. The fault lies partially with the barely adequate arrangements and the casual attitudes: Armstrong was no arranger himself, and was not much of a disciplinarian. He recorded popular tunes, some excellent such as "Stardust" and "Body and Soul," and many dull or awkward. Too many of his solos ended with a chorus of high note grandstanding. If his work in the thirties is not really as depressing as all these criticisms suggest, that is because of Armstrong's irrepressible genius, which still managed to make fine music out of "On Treasure Island" and "You Rascal You" and even, if the truth be known, out of "La Cucaracha." His singing, while continually entertaining, is not to be dismissed artistically: It influenced Billie Holiday, Ella Fitzgerald, Bing Crosby, Frank Sinatra, and a host of others.

There were some clear highlights of the thirties, including the vocal choruses on "When You're Smiling" and "After You've Gone." Armstrong was singing with the same kind of improvisatory freedom with which he played, and his gruff, gravel-filled voice is charming in its own way. He could be a very moving singer, as he demonstrated on two choruses of "On The Sunny Side of the Street," recorded in Paris in 1934, that build heartbreakingly. (A comparison with the same song recorded at Symphony Hall, Boston, in 1947 shows that this was something of a routine, but that does not diminish its power. In any case, as we have seen, such routines were common in early jazz.) His solo on "Sweethearts on Parade" (SCCJ) from 1930 includes a double-time quotation of the "High Society" clarinet solo, later to become a favorite of Charlie Parker. The two issued takes of "Stardust," made in 1931, show him improvising vocally and instrumentally, and repeating himself little. "Laughin' Louis" from 1933 is a treat, a vaudeville-style routine in which the band stops playing, but Armstrong jokes with them, and then continues with a majestic unaccompanied trumpet solo. (An alternate take first issued on CD shows that this recorded routine was not an accident, as previously believed.)

Armstrong remained a brilliant performer in the thirties, if a less startling one. His playing often sounded removed from the band which accompanied him. On arrangements such as "Hobo, You Can't Ride This Train" (1932), Armstrong seems to float over the band, riding his own rhythms in a manner that, though occasionally unnerving, is eerily effective: His rhythmic freedom sounds advanced even now.

After World War II, Armstrong returned to a small band. His personnel from 1947 through 1951 included such stars as Earl Hines, Jack Teagarden, New Orleans clarinetist Barney Bigard, and drummer Sid Catlett. Although the repertory became stale, these musicians didn't sound tired. A highlight of his

Members of Armstrong's All Stars around 1950: Earl
Hines on left, Jack Teagarden on right. (Courtesy
Rutgers Institute of Jazz Studies)

later career, and a significant event in the dissemination of jazz, was Armstrong's tours sponsored by the State Department in the late fifties. Armstrong especially treasured his reception in 1956 in Africa, where he was met by ecstatic crowds, carried on a litter, and danced to by a woman whom he said reminded him of his mother. One of his later records was aptly entitled *Ambassador Satch:* With his exuberance, independence and informality, he seemed to represent the best traits of American life.

He pleased huge crowds wherever he went, while being dismissed by some critics. Those dismissals seem hardly fair. He couldn't recapture the feeling of discovery that we hear in his music of his late twenties, but Armstrong continued to play and sing inimitably into his sixties. His "Sweet Lorraine" and "Just in Time" with Oscar Peterson from 1957 are joyous, subtle performances, as are "Solitude" and "It Don't Mean a Thing" with Duke Ellington from 1961. The live version of "Mahogany Hall Stomp" that became part of the movie *Satchmo the Great* opens with an ensemble chorus that, in its vibrant energy, rivals King Oliver's band. Armstrong's singing on "Atlanta Blues" and "Chantez-les-bas" from his 1954 recording of W.C. Handy songs is irresistible.

Armstrong had many rivals, even in the twenties, as record companies and managers scrambled to equal his popularity. These included Jabbo Smith, who played swift, elusive trumpet breaks with then unprecedented speed. "Sweet and Low Blues" (1929), a fascinating recording lauded by Schuller, features Smith's Armstrong-influenced vocals, and dazzling exchanges between Smith and clarinetist Omer Simeon. But Smith's career didn't take off.

A more durable rival was New Orleans-born Red Allen, whose father led a famous brass band, and whose early solos, as on "Biff'ly Blues" and "Feeling Drowsy" (1929), seem to combine something of Armstrong's warmth with the mysterious, "jungle" sound that was being popularized by Duke Ellington's brass players. Armstrong himself acknowledged one other rival, the fascinating Bix Beiderbecke. But the fact remains that Armstrong was the leading jazz musician of the twenties. Quite rightly he became virtually a symbol of jazz, of its roots in black culture, of its warmth and depth, and of its reach. Armstrong's music touched millions of lives throughout the world. It is not beyond criticism, but the best of it is, it seems to us, beyond praise.

7 Jazzin' in the Twenties

The twenties was a period of intense experimentation in jazz. By the end of the decade the music's vitality and importance were recognized, at least among musicians. Louis Armstrong was its acknowledged "king"—he seemed to influence every jazz musician, no matter on what instrument. In Chicago, a group of young white musicians were playing what might be called post-New Orleans improvisations. They had heard King Oliver live and found his band more compelling than the ODJB recordings which seemed to dominate much of the playing of white musicians elsewhere. But there were other innovators, and other traditions. Many of these emerged as the focus of the music gradually shifted to Chicago and then to New York City, where it has remained until the present. New York was the center of the music publishing and recording industry, as well as the biggest market for live jazz: there young white players like cornetist Red Nichols could make a career in the recording studios, and there pianists such as James P. Johnson had developed their own solo traditions. Although public performances by interracial groups were not accepted anywhere in America, a situation that changed slowly during World War II, black and white jazz artists influenced each other, played together in private, and recorded together. Musicians from all over were drawn to Manhattan. The twenties also saw the real beginning of the big band era. By the close of the decade, Armstrong would be playing with big bands exclusively, and a few years later, the style of the swing band era was in place in a few black bands. By the mid-thirties, swing would become the dominant style of jazz.

Of the cornetists who emerged in the twenties in Armstrong's wake, none was as original as Bix Beiderbecke, whose lyrical solos, each note clear as a bell, seemed to many to present an alternative to the more pressing style of Armstrong. Armstrong himself declared his admiration for Beiderbecke, and Bix would become the focus of an intense group of Chicago-based white musicians and eventually of musicians worldwide. His effect on them was startling. One of the Chicagoans, clarinetist Mezz Mezzrow, recalls Bix's playing, "every note full, big, rich and round, standing out like a pearl, loud but never irritating or jangling, with a powerful drive that few white musicians had in those days . . . The minute he started to blow I jumped with a flying leap into the harmony pattern . . . It was like slipping into a suit made to order for you by a fine tailor, silk-lined all through" (*Really the Blues*, pp. 68, 69).

Louis Armstrong, who jammed with Beiderbecke at least once, spoke of Bix's seriousness of purpose and of his marvelous tone. Tones might be more appropriate. Beiderbecke would push out a series of clarion notes, then pull back shyly, producing an almost muted sound. He could drive an ensemble with a series of repeated notes up high, or he might offer an offhand phrase behind another soloist as casually charming as his final choruses were dynamic. On those "outchoruses," he might suddenly explode, as in the pressured last chorus of "Goose Pimples" (1927). Bix's typical solos, even the short outings with the commercial Paul Whiteman orchestra, were lyrical, concise, modest but unforgettable.

Born in 1903, Beiderbecke had a staid upbringing in Davenport, Iowa. His mother did, however, play ragtime and Debussy on the family piano. Beiderbecke first heard jazz the way most midwesterners did, through the records of the ODJB. A natural pianist who could pick out tunes at the age of three and who later made a few memorable recordings on piano, Bix taught himself cornet, beginning by learning the ODJB's "Tiger Rag" on piano and then devel-

Bix Beiderbecke in 1923. (Courtesy Rutgers Institute of Jazz Studies)

oping a fingering on cornet that would allow him to play the notes. He never learned to finger the cornet conventionally. In 1919, Beiderbecke evidently heard Louis Armstrong on a Streckfus steamer boat that stopped in Davenport. By then, he was spending more time on music than on his studies. He was playing with high school bands, and he heard other jazz cornetists in person or on records, including Nick LaRocca of the Original Dixieland Jazz Band, Paul Mares of the New Orleans Rhythm Kings, the one-armed New Orleans native Wingy Manone, and a mysterious, because unrecorded, figure, Emmett Hardy. His parents, who wanted their son to become respectable, anything perhaps but a musician, lost patience, and in 1921 sent Bix to Lake Forest Academy, a private school north of Chicago.

They had unwittingly sent him to the place where jazz was developing fastest. Soon Beiderbecke was slipping down to Chicago to hear bands. Eventually these escapades resulted in his expulsion. By 1924, already recognized among Chicago musicians, Bix made his first recordings with a group named the Wolverines. One can hear something of Beiderbecke's originality even in these recordings. On numbers such as "Copenhagen," his lead playing seems both to float above the ensemble and to nudge it along graciously, like a practiced host moving his guests towards the dinner table. Even in 1924, his playing has none of the artificial jollity and jerky rhythms common in white Dixieland playing. But it wasn't until 1927, when Bix was playing with the Jean Goldkette orchestra, that he came into his own. Bix joined the Goldkette group in mid-1926 when it included some of the outstanding players of its day: violinist Joe Venuti, bassist Steve Brown, and C-melody saxophonist Frankie Trumbauer. Led by Trumbauer, for Goldkette was more of a booking agent than a musician, it became one of the most celebrated bands in the country, although it proved too expensive to maintain. The Goldkette band took on the leading black big band, Fletcher Henderson's, in a battle of bands at Roseland—a large club with an all-white clientele that often hired black and white bands to play alternate sets. By all accounts, Goldkette blew Henderson away. Cornetist Rex Stewart was with Henderson at the time, and he spoke of the engagement with characteristic generosity: "The facts were that we simply could not compete with Jean Goldkette's Victor Recording Orchestra. Their arrangements were too imaginative and their rhythm too strong, what with Steve Brown slapping . . . that bass fiddle and Frankie Trumbauer's inspiring leadership as he stood in front wailing with his C-melody saxophone" (Rex Stewart, *Jazz Masters of the Thirties*, p. 12). Later Henderson defeated the white Casa Loma band, a crack outfit, by, according to Stewart, playing Goldkette arrangements.

What made the Goldkette group stand out was these elaborate arrangements and the band's "freewheeling joy of playing with one another" (Stewart, p. 16). Unfortunately, while some of the arrangements were recorded, little of the joy was captured. Historians blame Victor executives who wanted popular hits rather than stunning jazz performances, and who thrust numbers like "I'm Gonna Meet My Sweetheart Now" and "Sunny Disposish" on the unwilling Goldkette musicians. While "My Pretty Girl" from February 1927 has something of the zest that impressed Rex Stewart, Beiderbecke was most prominently featured on recordings made that year with small groups led by Frankie Trumbauer. Trumbauer is best remembered for the sweet, liquid tone of his C-melody saxophone, his preferred instrument. (No longer used today, the C-melody saxophone was in size and sound between the alto and tenor saxophone.) On that instrument, Trumbauer took surprising solos whose unexpected leaps and harmonic sophistication revealed his musical kinship with Beiderbecke.

Beiderbecke and his circle were the first white players to have a significant influence as innovators, and they were widely admired by musicians of both races. One recording of Bix and Tram, as Trumbauer was known, changed jazz history. "Singin' the Blues" (SCCJ) was recorded on February 4, 1927. Trumbauer's opening solo was emulated by blacks and whites. According to Budd Johnson, "Everybody memorized that solo . . . At that time, Frankie Trumbauer was the baddest cat around" (*Down Beat*, February 8, 1968). Lester Young, later to become a leading influence in his own right, recalled for François Postif in 1959 the impact of that record when he was looking for a direction on the saxophone: "I had to make a decision between Frankie Trumbauer and Jimmy Dorsey. You dig? I wasn't sure which way I wanted to go, you dig? . . . The only people that was tellin' stories that I liked to hear were them . . . Did you ever hear him play "Singin' the Blues"? That tricked me right there, that's where I went." Impressed by Trumbauer's light tone, his graceful way of slurring notes, Young learned from Trumbauer's relaxed way of stating a melody and of playing around it. The example shows the solo that Trumbauer played over the skillful accompaniment of guitarist Eddie Lang. (See music example.)

The form of the 32-bar pop song underlying the piece is ABA'C, with in this case a solo break after the B section. Each section is eight bars and the second A section is slightly different from the first, thus A'. Trumbauer's first 16 bars use all the main notes of the written melody but he adds to that melody. After his sly break, he becomes more bluesy, beginning with an upward gesture similar to the one Bix will use in his solo. He ends with a rippling final run that introduces Bix. Bix then picks up from Trumbauer with an equally relaxed series of closely related phrases, played in his carefully regulated tone. He pushes out main notes and then pulls back as he moves towards a climactic upwards rip—a quick flashing glissando that was a stylistic feature of Armstrong's playing as well. Beiderbecke then falls away from the intensity implied by this rip, and finishes modestly. (This solo has been described in *Bix: Man and Legend*, by Richard Sudhalter and Richard Evans. This is the standard biography.) Almost as notable is the poised, gentle way the ensemble falls into line around Bix after his solo.

One of the innovations apparent on "Singin' the Blues" is in the rhythm section concept of the New York white players. There is no bass instrument on the recording, which is not unusual in itself, but instead one hears the prominent guitar of Eddie Lang playing contrapuntal lines and fills with the soloist, some of which are indicated in the music example. The drummers were subtle: During the final ensemble Chauncey Morehouse decorates the beat with cymbal

Example 7–1.
Frankie Trumbauer's solo on "Singin' the Blues" (1927), after a four-bar introduction.

splashes falling in delightfully unexpected places. Some of the clarinetists, such as Fud Livingston and especially Pee Wee Russell, eschewed the traditional virtuoso role, playing instead in a spare, even sly style. Here Jimmy Dorsey, often a virtuosic player, adopts the spare and witty approach for a deadpan eight bars near the end. This recording made its point: In 1931, Fletcher Henderson's band twice recorded "Singin' the Blues," in an arrangement probably by Gold-kette's Bill Challis. In it, Henderson's entire saxophone section recreated Trumbauer's solo, and cornetist Rex Stewart paid tribute to Beiderbecke.

In May 1927, Bix and Tram reentered the Okeh studios of New York repeatedly and recorded, among other numbers, "I'm Coming Virginia," with a brilliant entrance, all sunshine and grace, by Beiderbecke. Never in jazz had such modest means been used to such memorable effect. The form of "I'm Coming Virginia" is unusual. It consists of three eight-bar sections, AA'B. In this arrangement, the ensemble plays one chorus, which is followed by the verse played by Trumbauer. (As previously mentioned, twenties arrangements sometimes put the verse in the middle for variety.) Then Bix plays his first chorus accompanied primarily by, again, Lang's prominent guitar and Morehouse's dancing cymbals, with a few soft chords from the winds. While Bix has never been known as a blues player, he leans on the A-flat of the first solo measure—it's a "blue" note—bending it up and down, and in fact bends that note again in measures four and sixteen. One especially notices his light, tripping rhythms which breathe life into a stodgy melody. (See music example.)

Example 7–2.
Bix Beiderbecke's first chorus on "I'm Coming, Virginia."

For Bix's second chorus, he is joined by the winds throughout, improvising discreetly behind him, as he builds in intensity. Beiderbecke also took a long, lyrical solo on "Way Down Yonder in New Orleans." He sounded at the height of his powers and happy to be playing with his peers.

Nevertheless, he would soon enter the most controversial part of his career. The Goldkette orchestra in 1927 was failing rapidly: It would disband formally on September 18. Certain key members, including Bix and Tram and arranger Bill Challis, probably the most influential arranger in the twenties beside Don Redman, ended up in Paul Whiteman's band. Bix would spend most of the time that remained to him with Whiteman.

Advertised as "The King of Jazz," Paul Whiteman led the most extraordinarily successful large band of the twenties. Born in Denver in 1890, his father was a music educator and Paul was a classical violist before World War I. He began recording with a small dance band in August 1920. His first issued recording, "Whispering" with "Japanese Sandman" on its second side, was also his first hit. By mid-1923, its sales had reached well over a million. He had other hits as well and began recording prolifically. (The Whiteman story is told in *Pops: Paul Whiteman, King of Jazz* by Thomas A. DeLong.)

The group that recorded "Whispering" had nine musicians—or ten if you count a slide whistle soloist. By 1928, Whiteman's orchestra had grown to as many as 19 musicians, including strings, plus vocalists, making it larger than any jazz group. From the beginning, many of the Whiteman reed players played a variety of instruments—a Whiteman arrangement can call for flute, bass clarinet, bass sax, or an occasional bassoon. Whiteman was not a jazz musician, but he had an interest in jazz that impelled him to hire some of the best white jazz players he could find. Even before he managed to snare Beiderbecke, Whiteman had employed cornetist Red Nichols.

Whiteman is best known today for the Aeolian Hall concert in New York City on February 12, 1924, a concert which he called an "Experiment in Modern Music." The "experiment" began with a rendition of "Livery Stable Blues," and then a more recent jazz number, "Mama Loves Papa," which was described in the program as "written in the same slow rhythm which marks it as a jazz number," except that "it has been subdued and embellished so cleverly with a legitimate score that there is little that is offensive in it." Whiteman, then, was in the forefront of the movement to "make a lady out of jazz," as he put it. This concert ended with the premiere of a now famous work, "Rhapsody in Blue," an early essay in blending classical music with jazz. Its composer, George Gershwin, was at the piano. In 1930, Whiteman was the subject of the movie "King of Jazz." He continued as a bandleader throughout the thirties and beyond, and he continued his interest in mixing classical styles with jazz: Whiteman commissioned a variety of works for his orchestra, including a piece by Duke Ellington and the "Scherzo à la Russe" by Igor Stravinsky. He died in 1967.

When Beiderbecke went to Whiteman's band, he was joining a highly proficient, versatile orchestra which played arranged jazz as one of its many styles. On the day in 1928 that Whiteman recorded the pop song "Dardanella," with one of Bix's shining solos, the band also waxed three arrangements by its pianist Ferde Grofé, composer of the "Grand Canyon Suite": his version of "Oriental" by Granados, the "Meditation" of French opera composer Massenet, and "By the Waters of Minnetonka." Until the publication of *Bix: Man and Legend,* it was generally assumed that Bix was miserable in this band, unable to play lead, smothered by elephantine arrangements, forced to sit idly by while lesser men played novelty numbers.

In fact, Bix looked on the Whiteman band as "a terrific musical education," according to Jack Teagarden (*Bix: Man and Legend,* p. 254). When he sank into alcoholism, he deeply regretted having to leave Whiteman. Beiderbecke was in his personal life undisciplined, but, like other great jazz musicians, he was a curious man, in his own way an intellectual. Throughout the twenties he investigated classical music, French impressionists such as Ravel and Debussy, and American composers such as Edward MacDowell, the now largely forgotten

Eastwood Lane, and Gershwin. Gershwin, it should be noted, both influenced jazz musicians—Fats Waller quotes "Rhapsody in Blue" in his 1929 solo "Numb Fumblin' "—and was influenced by them. Gershwin was a virtuosic pianist who played at jazz parties, sometimes sitting in with Waller and others.

In the Whiteman band, Beiderbecke would learn to read more complicated parts than before, and he would be exposed to other knowledgeable musicians. His interest in modern classical music led him to compose gently impressionist piano pieces such as "In a Mist," which investigates harmonies no jazz band of the time was considering. Four of these pieces were published as sheet music: Beiderbecke recorded "In a Mist" as a piano solo in 1928. Whiteman, to his credit, was supportive in a way no other bandleader could have been: He presented Bix at a Carnegie Hall concert, playing "In a Mist" on a Steinway grand, accompanied discreetly by two other pianists.

Whiteman's arrangements were often carefully sculpted to set off Bix's cornet solos. Bill Challis, who had written for Bix in the Goldkette orchestra, used the wide range of possibilities that the Whiteman orchestra offered him. He wrote passages for three baritone saxophones, for tenor saxophone doubled by violins, for bassoon. Yet, unlike Grofé, whose taste was at times questionable, Challis used these possibilities chastely. His best arrangements, while not always fitting today's conceptions of jazz, are consistently vigorous, and full of intriguing effects, the most exciting of which is the sound of Bix's pristine cornet bursting out of an arranged passage in a short, enlivening solo. On "Changes," or "Back in Your Own Backyard," Beiderbecke's joyous or ardent statements are brilliantly prepared for by Challis. On "Changes" (BBJ), his 16 bars are played over the big-toned, pushy, swinging lines of Steve Brown, one of the great early string bassists. Bix emerges almost modestly from the ensemble of "Lonely Melody" and then offers one of his most lyrical statements, while during "From Monday On" he leaps out of the ensemble startlingly. (See music example.)

Example 7–3.
Bix Beiderbecke, first 8 bars of his solo on "From Monday On." This is the correct key; many reissues play in A.

(This is the recording from February 13, 1928. There are two different takes from February 28, 1928.) Challis recognized the value of Bix and Tram. His version of "You Took Advantage of Me" ends with a cool duet by Beiderbecke and Trumbauer, whose movements are as suavely intertwined as in a dance by Fred Astaire and Ginger Rogers.

Most of the Whiteman numbers with Bix were recorded by Victor, but in May of 1928, the band moved to Columbia. The Columbia recordings, often of inferior material, coincide with Beiderbecke's personal decline. But they have their moments, as when on "That's My Weakness Now" Bix follows the written lead trumpet of Charlie Margulis with a brilliant solo: Like Duke Ellington, as will be seen, Challis made use of the contrasting sounds and styles of his trumpet players. On " 'Tain't So, Honey, 'Tain't So" (June 1928), Bix plays a brief muted solo, then is given an open cornet passage: He sounds like two men. The best of Bix with Whiteman is as lyrical, as charming in a bright-eyed modest way, as anything in jazz. His experiments came to an abrupt close. Bix died at the age of 28 in 1931, a victim of alcohol-induced pneumonia.

RED NICHOLS AND OTHER WHITE INNOVATORS

Beiderbecke's influence on other, especially white, jazzmen was profound. In New York, cornetist Red Nichols, after listening to the ODJB, had arrived at a style similar to Bix's before he heard Beiderbecke. But there is no question that Bix's influence was definitive once Nichols had heard the "young man with a horn," as the Dorothy Baker novel (and film) inspired by Beiderbecke called its hero. Nichols seemed to be everywhere in New York in the twenties. Like many of the white jazzmen he worked with, Nichols worked as a studio musician for recordings and radio, and as a jazzman. He also recorded regularly as a leader, employing a different repertory than black groups of the day, concentrating

Red Nichols and his Five Pennies around 1926. From left: Nichols, Jimmy Dorsey, Bill Haid (replacing Arthur Schutt, the usual pianist), Vic Berton (with tympani), Miff Mole, Eddie Lang. (Courtesy Rutgers Institute of Jazz Studies)

mostly on originals and vaudeville tunes, and songs by the likes of Hoagy
Carmichael, and including relatively fewer blues or rags.

Much of what Nichols did was innovative, even self-consciously experimental. He used clever, complex arrangements with unusual instrumentation.
Cooler than Armstrong's and less surprising than Beiderbecke's, his solos sound
planned. (Curiously, he frequently sounded most relaxed as a soloist when he
was with the Whiteman orchestra, rather than on his own.) Although his solos
do not burst with energy, they contain some advanced effects. Nichols used the
recording studio to present experimental material. But he did not continue to
experiment during his later career. Nichols led a relatively sedate big band in the
thirties, and then later travelled with his successful Dixieland group. In 1959, his
life was the subject of a Hollywood film starring Danny Kaye.

Red Nichols and His Five Pennies recorded Hoagy Carmichael's "Boneyard
Shuffle" in 1926 for Brunswick Records. The group features Eddie Lang on
guitar, Vic Berton on percussion, Arthur Schutt on piano, Miff Mole on trombone and Jimmy Dorsey on alto saxophone and clarinet. Again there is no bass.
In this fast-paced arrangement, the song is transformed by numerous complicated breaks and changes in rhythmic style. Whole-tone scales show up in the
solos (such as Dorsey's alto break in the middle of his opening solo) and in the
writing. French composer Claude Debussy had inspired a whole generation of
impressionist composers with his innovative scale, and these jazz players were
enamored of it as well. (See music example.)

Example 7–4.
Whole-tone scales—each note is a whole-tone apart.

Berton takes melodic breaks on tympani—the first use of that instrument in
recorded jazz. His playing throughout is delightful. He fills in for the missing
bass, and, at the start of Mole's trombone solo he, pianist Schutt, and Nichols
(softly) play a kind of pre-rhythm and blues pattern together based on the
popular Charleston dance beat of the day (See music example).

Example 7–5.
From "Boneyard Shuffle," rhythm played behind the trombone solo.

Berton gets the effect of a high-hat—before it was available—by using a stick to hit the cymbal which he then damps with his other hand. (A high-hat is a device that hits two cymbals together when a foot pedal is depressed. Its use became widespread around 1930.)

Miff Mole's solo is, in its graceful seriousness, far ahead of most other trombonists of the time. His style is full of graceful leaps and a striking kind of wit. He was probably familiar with the virtuoso trombonist Arthur Pryor, who was prominently featured, with Sousa's band and then his own, playing with superlative fluency on ragtime-derived pieces. Mole's influence is evident in a few other recordings, such as black trombonist Eddie Durham's first work with the Benny Moten band, and Mole was respected for his technical ability. And Jimmy Dorsey was probably the most skillful saxophone player yet involved in jazz. Like Trumbauer, Dorsey was influenced by the famous light classical and ragtime virtuoso, Rudy Wiedoeft. Dorsey was not necessarily a great natural improvisor. As alternate takes demonstrate, both Dorsey and Nichols prepared solos which they repeated almost note for note.

Nichols was prolific. He made more records per year than Louis Armstrong—and he assembled the best white jazz musicians for his recordings. In 1929, Nichols recorded "Basin Street Blues" with a totally different group that included three Chicagoans—the fine drummer Dave Tough, Joe Sullivan on piano, Bud Freeman on tenor—as well as Pee Wee Russell on clarinet, and Jack Teagarden on trombone and voice. (The group was fancifully billed as the Louisiana Rhythm Kings.) The number became a feature for Teagarden, one of the most compelling jazz trombonists.

Teagarden eschewed Mole's more staccato style. Together with his friend, the less well known black trombonist Jimmy Harrison who played with Fletcher Henderson, Teagarden transformed the jazz trombone, playing the previously unwieldy horn with a legato grace and ease, and a depth of feeling, that was unprecedented. His nonchalant phrasing, elegant use of grace notes and lip trills (trills made by adjusting the lips rather than moving the hands), smooth melodic passages, and virtuosic codas proved that the trombone could be as expressive as any instrument. Teagarden prepared the way for the swing era stardom of Tommy Dorsey, Jimmy's younger brother, and Glenn Miller, both in the late twenties disciples of Teagarden.

Teagarden was born in Vernon, Texas in 1905, and taught himself trombone, developing his own lip techniques and special slide positions to accomodate his short arms. "That was one of the secrets of his tremendous fast technique," said his brother, trumpeter Charlie, "because he didn't play it like a trombone at all. If you'll talk to other trombone players who ever saw him play, they could never figure out what . . . he was doing, because he never got past the bell, he never got down in the low register at all."

As a child, he played hymns in church, and heard black spiritual music from a revival tent next door to his house. Perhaps because of this exposure, Teagarden was at home with the blues, both as an instrumentalist, and, which was more rare for a white musician, as a singer. He may be the premiere white